Soul Reunion

Understanding Where We Came From,
Embracing Who We Are

Laura Ann Day

WestBow
PRESS
A DIVISION OF THOMAS NELSON

Copyright © 2011 Laura Ann Day

All rights reserved. No part of this book may be used or reproduced by any means, graphic, electronic, or mechanical, including photocopying, recording, taping or by any information storage retrieval system without the written permission of the publisher except in the case of brief quotations embodied in critical articles and reviews.

WestBow Press books may be ordered through booksellers or by contacting:

WestBow Press
A Division of Thomas Nelson
1663 Liberty Drive
Bloomington, IN 47403
www.westbowpress.com
1-(866) 928-1240

Because of the dynamic nature of the Internet, any web addresses or links contained in this book may have changed since publication and may no longer be valid. The views expressed in this work are solely those of the author and do not necessarily reflect the views of the publisher, and the publisher hereby disclaims any responsibility for them.

Any people depicted in stock imagery provided by Thinkstock are models, and such images are being used for illustrative purposes only.

Certain stock imagery © Thinkstock.

ISBN: 978-1-4497-1447-5 (sc)
ISBN: 978-1-4497-1448-2 (dj)
ISBN: 978-1-4497-1449-9 (e)

Library of Congress Control Number: 2011924773

Printed in the United States of America

WestBow Press rev. date: 3/24/2011

*For Brooklyn, Carter, Savannah, Brayden and Kaylee.
And for every "grand" yet to come.
All My Love,
Ni*

Acknowledgements

First and foremost, I give thanks to God from whom all blessings flow! Through the exercise of developing this project from a small 40-day study into a full-fledged book, God has moved His words and His purpose through my work. Let it be understood that I never wish to lead with my own thoughts or fancies. To God be all glory and power and dominion, forever.

I want to thank my husband, Robert, whose encouragement and support has been stalwart. His ability to never flinch even when fiery darts are thrown directly in his path is an inspiration to me. He has never doubted this book would be completed, and tolerated mood swings, writer's block and frozen dinners with very little complaining. You are the love of my life, Robert, and the true mate of my heart.

Thanks also to my children—both my natural born and my "daughters-in-love"—without whom I would have never found the courage to try. Their tenacity and determination in pursuing their own goals, their hard fought victories and their strength in facing their own challenges has left me in awe. They have taught me to never give up on my dreams, and have circled the wagons in the times of our greatest challenges. Robby, Kami, Brian, Chelce, Ashley, and Anna, you are my joy! (The grand children are definitely the icing on the cake!)

Thanks to my parents-in-love, Earl and Sarah Day. Their example of Christ in action and their attitudes of complete servanthood humble me beyond words. They have shown me how to put others above myself and how to honor God with my life.

To my whole family, near and far, thank you for showing me through your example what loyalty and honor look like. As different we all are, we are astonishingly united. I will never forget the lessons.

To Mary Francis Roebuck and Colleen Wait, thank you for being smarter than my spell-check.

I must send thanks to the many people who have inspired me through the years, and shown me the importance of faith, family and friendship…

To Anna and Darrell Hewett, who have shown me the true essence of perseverance and the embodiment of walking with God.

To my many mentors: Loretta Parrish, Larry and Linda Cline, James Moore, Dudley Chancey, and Gary and Zoe Lambrecht. Thank you for always having time to guide me and share your wisdom. It has not gone unnoticed, and I am deeply thankful for your help. You've steadied me and loved with true *"agapeo."*

To my sister-shield-maidens, who have stood on the front lines with me, through thick and thin, and have prayed protection over me in my harshest battles: Audrey Stevens, Sheila Lowe, Paige Myers, the entire "Daughters of the King" staff, Linda Munson, Nicole Jones, Carol Stringfellow, Tese Stutzman, Zo Clendenin, Andrea Hermann, Jamie Lambrecht Hermann, Casma Henlon, Ernestine Moss, Kelly Stefanko, Yvonne Kotchman, Desh Begley, Debbie Baker, Karen Fanning, Tanza Pride, and Beulla McHale. NO WAY would this have happened without you sword-swinging ladies! It is amazing what a girl can do when her sisters have her back.

Lastly, thank you to the elders of my home congregation, the Bay Area Church of Christ. Thank you for every opportunity to teach and serve. Your confidence in me is invaluable. You have drawn my boundaries in the most pleasant places, a gift of trust I have never before enjoyed to such an extent. I pray that I have honored your trust and confidence, and that this will be the first of many projects God entrusts to us. I greatly admire all of you.

I pray that God will bless all of you beyond your wildest imagination. I love you dearly.

Contents

Forward		xiii
Preface		xvii
Introduction		xix
Chapter 1	Home	1
Chapter 2	Love Is…	13
Chapter 3	Destinations and Detours	21
Chapter 4	Changing Course	31
Chapter 5	The Rainbow… AFTER The Rain	39
Chapter 6	Leaving Home	51
Chapter 7	A New Name	61
Chapter 8	The Waiting	73
Chapter 9	The Other Side of Danger	85
Chapter 10	The Impossible & The Impassible	97
Chapter 11	When Faith Is All You Have	105
Chapter 12	Be Prepared	113
Chapter 13	The Pictures	123

Forward

Have you ever been in a room full of people when you suddenly feel a charge in the energy level? You don't even have to turn around to know that someone new has entered the room; someone with such positivity that their smile and personality sends electric currents throughout the group. Laura is such an individual!

Life is an adventure for Laura, and I am proud to be Ethel to her Lucy and Laverne to her Shirley. We have skipped down the road of life together, skillfully wriggling ourselves into and out of every conceivable curve life can throw at two crazy women. We have laughed, cried, prayed, and like the iconic *Golden Girls*, we have discovered that some of life's best answers are found while sharing cheesecake and conversation. Time and time again I have marveled at the grace and dignity with which she has navigated obstacles. With total dependence and complete reliance on God, she fully submits to His will in her life.

In *Soul Reunion*, Laura invites us on a personal journey where her passion for relationships is integrated with her passion for living within God's sovereignty. Here she clearly illustrates how our adversities are <u>*God's opportunities*</u>. Laura brings a fresh perspective and renewed energy to the stories we have treasured since infancy. Through moving encounters with people of the

Bible, this book affirms that God can move you along on your journey with power and clarity.

Somewhere between the pages of this book and the pages of your heart God is calling you to a Soul Reunion. Don't miss your reservation!

Audrey Stevens, Dallas, Texas
Co-Founder, Daughters of the King Girls' Conference

Over the years I have know Laura, we have enjoyed many mealtimes together. There is something somewhat intimate when you actual "share" a meal as opposed to just eating next to someone. One particular mealtime stands out from the rest...

As a part of the *Daughter's of the King* team, I was flying into Dallas for our first all-girls youth conference in Texas. Several of the crew spent most of the day collecting each staff member as their planes landed, and my plane was the last to arrive from our group. The post-airport plan was for everyone to enjoy a nice dinner together, perhaps indulging in a legendary Texas-size steak or world famous Tex-Mex spread.

Well as plans and planes don't always cooperate, the seven of us ended up in Audrey's van, individually leaning across the driver calling out our order to the box under the Sonic menu hoping the tasty collection of fried items would arrive before we all passed out from lack of sustenance. Once the girl on roller skates with the adorable accent showed up, the fun began. Our crew was finally back together and the reminiscing, storytelling and laughter soon flowed in abundance. Our *Soul Reunion* had begun!

In this book, Laura invites you to a different dinner table of sorts. She has gathered some of our Christian family's "Who's Who" to reminisce and story tell. Don't worry, there will be plenty of laughter and as with all families, plenty of tears. You will close the book knowing a little more about your Christian heritage, a little more about yourself and a whole lot more about your Father and that amazing Brother of ours.

Laura doesn't claim to know all the answers to life, she simply opens her heart up to you, shares the questions she has asked along the way and gives God the glory when He guides her to the next chapter. In my 20 years of ministering to teens and women, I've never met a more determined and humble servant. Laura has faced each challenge excited about the way God was going to grow her through. I am thrilled she finally carved out the time to put it down in words and you are truly privileged to hold it in your hands!

Come and join her at the table, "all things are ready, come to the feast."

Sheila Lowe, Holly Hill Church of Christ
Keynote, Daughters of the King Girls' Conference

Preface

So much can happen in just two short years. When I began this project in 2008, it was in the form of a forty-day study for a very small group of women at my home congregation. At that time, there was growing desire within the female sector of our family to be more significantly connected to their place in God's kingdom. We were beginning a time of prayer and fasting in an effort to rid ourselves of our own agendas and sweep our spiritual house clean of anything in opposition to God's will for us. Our hope was that by leaving our heart-space wide open, God would fill it with HIS PLANS.

Because the process was so powerful within our small number, we offered the study more broadly to all women in the congregation later that year. To our delight and surprise, some of our men chose to participate, and several families decided to do the study together as well. God moved so very powerfully within the lives of those who committed to the process of God's refinement that it was requested that I teach a class on this same subject at the beginning of 2010, taking more time to really examine the stories referenced in Hebrews 11 & 12. The hope was that we would come to more fully understand our spiritual lineage and more fully embrace our place within these spiritual generations.

At the conclusion of our study, an elder in our church approached me with a challenge: put the study into book form. The final product is in your hands.

There is so much more that happened within this process, too much to include in these pages. The abridged version is that my family faced some gut-wrenching challenges during this time. To say that God is the only thing that held us through the storms is such an inadequate statement. I see now that God used the time we spent together composing the forty-day study to prepare me to be a true student of His word and to develop a deep hunger within me to really understand His teachings. Then He used my time of study and fasting to prepare me for the tsunami-like burdens that arrived immediately following the conclusion of the forty days.

Lastly, God used the unity found with those who participated with me as a resource for fellow prayer warriors in my time of great need. I know for certain I would have never made it through—so astonishingly unscathed—had they not been willing to bear the shield and wield the sword on my behalf. They were truly my rear guard.

I am convinced this book is meant to be. The message within its chapters stands in powerful and unyielding opposition to the dark forces of this world. I am blessed daily with a peace that God is completely in control regardless of the circumstances swirling about me. I arrived at this place through this editorial exercise: Mind, body and spirit only desiring to glorify The One who created me for this very time, and for this very purpose.

Praise to God! Honor and glory to Him alone! Blessings and thanksgiving to my redeemer, Jesus Christ!

Introduction

Welcome to your *Soul Reunion*!

This book is designed in such a way that anyone can benefit from its lessons. While it is non-fiction as opposed to study booklet format, it is still for the use of broadening one's knowledge and understanding of Biblical scripture, as well as application to daily living.

As such, it is strongly suggested that as you read, you should also have a New International Version of the Bible at hand, or the translation of your personal preference. There will be numerous times when it will be tremendously beneficial (or completely necessary) to read the full story referenced within the lesson so as to have a complete vision of the information being covered. Because each chapter has a section entitled, *Points to Ponder*, it is also suggested to have a notebook available to use as a journal as you reflect on and answer the questions.

If using *Soul Reunion* as a quarterly classroom study or a book club selection, each person should be prepared to discuss those questions presented at the end of the chapters. While personal introspection can do some good, the experience, wisdom and perspective of those sharing this journey may prove to be invaluable. Always bear in mind that God does not do things haphazardly and He does not make mistakes. Those with whom you are studying are there for the purpose of your growth, as you are there for theirs.

May God bless you as you enter this walk with Him. May grace and peace come to all who take a seat at His table. Glory and renown be to The One who called us to the feast.

Chapter 1

Home

[Greek-] OIKOS: *of royalty- palace *of deity- temple *family-lineage, people who originated in a specific household

Let me begin by confessing some things to you, the reader. I love family gatherings. I love reunions of all sizes for any and every reason. My family, both immediate and extended, is incredibly precious to me. Gathering together and sharing life not only binds us together in the "now" of things; it connects us to all the generations of the past through stories, traditions, and even recipes. The gathering is the glue, if you will.

Yes, my family is definitely precious. This is not to imply that we are lovely and perfect in every way. Make no mistake; the lot of us is a conglomeration of a hot mess. We put the "fun" in dysfunctional. That is what I love about us. Take any one of us to examine under a microscope and you're definitely going to find some "stuff." I'm certain the stuff is a dominant gene, because no matter how far back in the lineage one continues the search…Look! There's the stuff! But no matter what our faults, shortcomings, or differences, through politics and personalities, we genuinely enjoy being together. Which brings me to another sentiment…

I love weddings. Two lives becoming one, facing an uncertain future with confidence – weddings are the embodiment of new beginnings. Beginnings carry hope and promise and infinite dreams. Not a sad thought or negative whim is present in the hearts of the couple, only possibilities.

This past summer we had the pleasure of witnessing many weddings, two of which were in our immediate family. Each ceremony was a unique and very appropriate reflection of the couple being united in marriage. They've all been so much fun that I haven't even minded the depleted bank account, the result of what we now refer to as "The Summer of the Five-Piece Place Settings."

One wedding was small, intimate and low key. The groom's grandfather officiated; siblings plus a handful of close friends were attendants. One of my daughters was a bridesmaid, and there was a reunion of sorts of all the high school cross-country kids with their long-tenured and now-retired coach. That was a precious moment for everyone. Can you imagine the collective number of training miles standing on that dance floor? The parallel for the couple was obvious: you can go the distance.

There was my niece's wedding. It was a fairly large Deep South celebration that included many attendants, a long walk down a beautiful church aisle and several children doing the many adorably imperfect things for which flower girls and ring bearers are famous. The bride, the youngest and only girl of four children, was given to her groom not only by her father and mother, but also by her older brothers. This could have taken a very mafia-esque turn for the worse; thankfully the boys behaved themselves, and it was a precious moment, just as intended. I'm sure the food, dancing and revelry will be remembered. I'm also 100 percent certain the blown transformer, no electricity, no air conditioning, a fire alarm screaming moments prior to the wedding procession,

and the mother and sister-in-law of the bride getting stuck in an elevator will become epic stories for generations to come.

Most memorable, though, was my second cousin's wedding in the Washington DC area. My husband and I flew from our home in Florida to the Baltimore airport, and promptly began our usual struggle for alpha status beginning at the rental car counter. I handled all the arrangements, and Mr. Control continually peppered me with irrelevant questions as I was just trying to get my hands on the keys and a map. I still don't understand how anyone thinks men are incapable of multi-tasking. My male did just fine simultaneously injecting himself into a conversation he knew nothing about while checking emails, making business calls and downloading new applications to his phone. I even give him bonus points for charming a toddler in the mix. Well, maybe not. He is inherently charming anyway, so doing that which comes naturally might not count. After all, would he give me credit for falling in love with really cute shoes?

As we loaded our bags into the trunk it seemed as if our attitudes were headed straight down the tubes. In an effort to stop the madness we declared détente and vowed to speak more kindly, lest the weekend be completely ruined. This is not to infer that anyone who has control issues actually surrendered control. Clearly not receiving the information I repeatedly tried to convey, Mr. Control harped that we must stop at a drive-thru for lunch so as to not unduly impose on our hosts immediately upon our arrival. I tried to remind him of the traditions and customs of my family. We're big, we're loud, and we're fairly certain *My Big Fat Greek Wedding* was created via hidden camera footage from my parents' 50th Anniversary bash. Also, we eat. We eat big. We love lavish, we love delicious, we love *dining*! To be exact, when word gets out that our clan is having a major event or celebration, caterers everywhere rejoice. Still, rather than argue I swung into a burger joint, grabbed the goods and continued our drive.

Fifteen minutes later, we walked up to the front door of my cousin's home, which promptly flung open into a joyously

Laura Ann Day

screaming multitude of hugs and kisses. We were passed around like a shiny new toy at Christmas, hugs flying, cameras flashing with the fervor of paparazzi in pursuit of a prize celebrity. When we finally had a chance to stand still I noticed my husband's dumbfounded expression. I followed his gaze, which rested right smack dab in the middle of the kitchen on the large granite island…overflowing with every kind of food imaginable.

And there it was: The Moment.

There was the very moment I knew I was *home*. There was the beautiful epiphany when every cloud of frustration seemed to part and the rays of gleaming vindication filled my world. There was the moment I understood that this is my territory, my history, *mia familia*, my POSSE! There was the moment when all past generations of southern hospitality intersected with my immediate need for application otherwise known as, "I told you so."

To the untrained eye this whole scenario might seem trivial. It wasn't. It's important to understand that no amount of verbal mind jogging succeeded in my efforts to make my husband understand that his hunger needs would be satisfied, and with flourish! He had to walk right up to it and see the evidence face to face. Learning a lesson this way is invaluable. The imprinting of it in one's mind can only be achieved through experiential learning. Believe me, this man will never doubt again!

The full impact of that weekend extended far beyond that initial "aha moment." We will treasure each and every moment spent in the presence of this crazed mob. Mealtimes were abundant and sumptuous, loud and long. Each featured a combination of new dishes contributed by various people as well as long standing back-in-the-day favorites. Those favorites were presented with all the pomp and circumstance they deserved, and all in attendance scrambled for a peek at the hand-written recipe card or dog-eared page. So many memories, happy and sad, are bound up in these dishes. If they could speak, oh what stories they'd tell. The loving hands that prepared them for our enjoyment are the same hands in our family that have held us together through

divorces, illness, unemployment and loss. These same hands have cheered our accomplishments, prayed for our strength and gently steadied toddlers' steps. This weekend was an aria of old meets new, past meets present; here is where a blend of many yesterdays nodded towards tomorrow. It was like the life-weathered hands of grandparents being instinctively grasped by fresh newborn fingers, wisdom and knowledge greeting hope and promise.

It was perfection.

I have come to have immeasurable appreciation for such gatherings. The time spent listening to the stories of who we are and where we came from have become the threads of our family's tapestry, each narrative lending color, depth and dimension to my understanding of how I became the person I am today. More importantly, it has revealed my connection to every past generation and reinforced the relevance of my own life-threads' binding within the weave. I understand that even the darkest colors have purpose in the loom and produce dramatic framing to the contrasting bright threads of life. The more tightly the threads are woven together, the stronger our fabric becomes. Although it will always be a work in progress, our family tapestry is an incredible work of art.

God has been so gracious to me in the past few months in this same way. I have been blessed to explore the *Faith of the Ancients* as found in the book of Hebrews, chapters 11 & 12. Each story referenced is rich and textured, and completely relevant to the application of holy living in this challenging world. Examining the threads of our biblical lineage helps us understand where we came from, who we are, and how we ourselves are bound in the weaving of the family of faith. Here we discover our connection to God's purpose and our importance to His plan.

Every new generation searches for insights in God's scripture. Most begin their spiritual journey believing theirs will be the generation that rocks the foundations of the church with their indictments of the past and its scandals, and their enlightening revelations for the future. Herein lies the irony that cannot be ignored: we all must look closely at the past, receiving and embracing its lessons, if we want to face the future with confidence and clothe ourselves in the hope that sustains through the ages. The more tightly we bind ourselves to understanding our past, the stronger we ultimately become.

Cynics say history is bound to repeat itself. But anyone can change his destiny if he is bound in devotion to God, through His son and our Savior Jesus Christ! Ignorant, thoughtless words of the visionless masses are no match for the God whose words have the power to speak things into existence. The God we serve provides fullness and completeness for all who choose to follow closely in the steps of our patriarchs. Where is the best place to start? In the beginning…

So now, just like my husband had to experience walking directly into generations of history in the form of a banquet table, let's take a walk with those who have gone before us. God has prepared a feast for our hearts and souls. You've been hungry, and He has been cooking old "family" recipes for a long, long time eagerly anticipating your presence at this table. Welcome home!

"In the Beginning:"

Powerful Words with Potent Possibilities

When the author of the book of Hebrews penned his letter to primarily Jewish converts, the purpose was to reiterate what had been previously taught: Jesus Christ is supreme and completely sufficient as the mediator and administrator of God's grace and salvation.

The recipients of this letter were completely familiar with the path by which Jesus arrived. Remember, these are Jews. From generation to generation, stories and prophecies that embodied their religious practices were taught everywhere in their environment. So when confusion arose concerning how this new

religious doctrine should be practiced, this writer knew the very best place to go for resolution: In the beginning.

> *"Now faith is being sure of what we hope for and certain of what we do not see. This is what the ancients were commended for. By faith we understand that the universe was formed at God's command, so that what is seen was not made out of what is visible."* (Hebrews 11:1-3)

These words call us to travel back to creation. Genesis 1:1 says:

> *"In the beginning, God created the heavens and the earth."*

There is so much benefit in reviewing what is already known. The author knew that calling to mind the lessons taught to each Hebrew from infancy not only would bring order and calm, but also comfort. If the Gospel is Nouveau-Cuisine for this crowd, then these Old Testament stories are comfort food. These folks were escorted into Abba Father's kitchen and invited to partake in the most traditional family fare. Here in Hebrews 11:1- 12: 13, the author spreads their spiritual table with the same feast that had been enjoyed by so many previous generations. Each recollection is anchored in this people's principle understanding of the word "faith," which is from the Greek *"pisteuo."* This word carries the express implication that actions based on faith, (trust, belief) will follow from the one who possesses it. And so he begins,

> *"By faith Abel offered a better sacrifice…"*
> *"By faith Enoch was taken from this life… he was commended as one who pleased God."*
> *"By faith Noah, when warned about things not yet seen, in holy fear built an ark to save his family."*
> *"By faith Abraham, when called to go to a place he would later receive as an inheritance, obeyed and went, even though he did not know where he was going."*

> "By faith Abraham, even though he was past age—and Sarah herself was barren—was enabled to become a father because he considered him faithful who had made the promise."
>
> "By faith Abraham, when God tested him, offered Isaac as a sacrifice. He who had received the promises was about to sacrifice his one and only son, even though God said to him 'It is through Isaac that your offspring will be reckoned.'"
>
> "By faith Isaac blessed Jacob & Esau in regard to their future."
>
> "By faith Jacob, when he was dying, blessed both of Joseph's sons…"
>
> "By faith Joseph, when his end was near, spoke about the exodus of Israelites from Egypt…"
>
> "By faith Moses' parents hid him for three months after he was born, because they saw he was no ordinary child, and they were not afraid of the King's edict."
>
> "By faith Moses, when he had grown up, refused to be known as the son of Pharaoh's daughter. He chose to be mistreated along with the people of God…"
>
> "By faith the people passed through the Red Sea on dry land…"
>
> "By faith the walls of Jericho fell…"
>
> "By faith the prostitute Rahab, because she welcomed the spies, was not killed with those who were disobedient."
>
> "…These were commended for their faith, yet none of them received what had been promised. God planned something better for us, so that only together with us would they be made perfect."

This particular generation was the last in a long line that had waited so long for Messiah. When He finally came, they mistakenly thought they had reached their final destination, a mindset common among Christians even today. We view the moment of our conversion as a destination, someplace we have to get to. We take on an air of relief that we finally have "that"

taken care of. In truth, when we commit to a life with Christ as our Lord, it is, most definitively, our beginning. It may be beneficial, then, to look more closely at the original language of these scriptures for the meaning conveyed in the beginning. While the English language is both complex and expressive, it can fall short from full potency of what was originally intended. What, exactly, were the ancients commended for?

Here are some definitions.

FAITH: [Greek-] pisteuo/pistis= faith, belief, trust; with an implication that actions based on this trust will follow.

SURE: [Greek-] hypostasis= confidence, trust

HOPE: [Greek-] elpizo= to hope, to hope for, put hope in, expect; an attitude of confidently looking forward to what is good and beneficial

ANCIENTS: [Greek-] presbyteros= older, ancestral

COMMENDED: [Greek-] martyreo= to testify, to give testimony; commend, speak well of, vouch for;

{Another derivative/extension- martyria, which is a person whose life is a testimony or evidence}

UNIVERSE: [Greek-] aion= eternity, time period, age

FORMED: [Greek-] katartizo= to restore, put in order, to make complete, to prepare, ordain, equip

COMMAND: [Greek-] rhema= word, saying, charge

CREATE: [Hebrew-] bara= create; Creator; refers to creating from nothing as well as re-forming existing materials.

{NOTE: The verb is of profound theological significance, since it only has GOD as it's subject. The verb precisely expresses ONLY GOD can create in the sense implied by bara.}

So, according to Hebrews 11:1-3, and Genesis 1:1, those who have gone before us (our elders, ancestors) have left a trail of evidence to be examined. Without having anything that could be seen ahead of time but accepting the events of their lives as proof that God is always provident and completely powerful, they chose a lifestyle based on trust in God. They confidently expected *(elpizo)* that following God was good and beneficial.

Their testimony, shared from generation to generation, pointed directly to the evidence that God literally spoke the words that formed their time period. They fully accepted without question that He gave it order, making it complete in every way. Their actions were based on the acceptance that He gave everything in existence a place and a purpose ordained by God, Himself. Their lives, thoughts and actions were grounded in acceptance of God as their Creator, their seat of life and the source of all existence, and acknowledging that without Him there is no life.

Points to Ponder

Take some time to meditate on these:
- How do you think *your* life would change if you fully accepted that your very existence is only possible because God ordained it?
- How would your direction change if you surrendered your whole life, laying it bare for God, allowing Him to order it in such a way that you became "evidence" for those who came after you?
- Can we actually give up personal agendas?

It will be easy to rationalize this moment away. After all, you have programs to be introduced. You have a vision for new activities. If you don't get the orders for new curriculum done, then who will? What about the daytime job? Aren't you allowed to have a life? You have to be organized or your life will spin out of control. Listen, friend, I've been by this drive-through before. You're not in control anyway. I can assure you of this: anything you may have <u>*in your mind*</u> or <u>*on your list*</u> will pale by comparison to all that God can reveal to you through <u>surrender</u>. Anything we can possibly conceive in our minds is merely junky fast food for the impatient; all the while a feast has been readied to satisfy

your deepest hunger for purpose and relevance. Revival awaits those who can surrender. Renewal is free to all who will submit themselves to a time of God's transformation. It has worked for many generations with a lifetime guarantee for effectiveness.

It's sure to leave you dumbfounded.

> *"Since ancient times*
> *no one has heard,*
> *No ear has perceived,*
> *No eye has seen any God besides you,*
> *Who acts on behalf of those…*
> *who wait for him."*
> *(Isaiah 64:4)*

Chapter 2

Love Is…

I'm not sure when we crossed the line from uncomfortable to comical. Our first clue should have been that the ushers had nothing to do. Did I mention that one of the weddings we attended was outdoors? The setting was a gorgeous garden area in Alexandria, Virginia, overlooking the Potomac River. It was beautiful. Let me rephrase that. It was beautiful looking at it from the window of the historic farmhouse, which was air-conditioned. No one, it seemed, was in any way motivated to leave the comfort of the industrially cooled indoors to take their seats in the garden for the main event, hence the idle ushers. The inevitable hour arrived, however, and we were summoned by an extremely polite yet sweat soaked groomsman to make our way to our chairs so the ceremony could begin. Of course we obliged. It was, after all, the intentional reason for the weekend.

Mr. Control's tush had barely found its landing before the hushed conference with his other male allies began: We're taking our suit jackets off, are you in? In unison, off the jackets went and the battle lines were drawn against the swelter. It was a futile attempt to stave off the atmospheric assault. The collective army of stiffly starched dress shirts was no match for the overpowering heat. Within three minutes of our arrival, the music, the wedding procession and the surrender to perspiration commenced. The poor kid two seats down even leaned forward so the sweat wouldn't drip on his tie.

The one and only comfort in our surrender was this: Here comes our bride. Oh, she was absolutely radiant, and not from the heat! From the moment she arrived to the final kiss, she completely captivated every heart in her wake. This is why we came. This is what made it all worth it. The purity and beauty of a wedding is what we came to participate in. The process by which two physical bodies and two distinctly unique souls are united as one through a pledge of commitment is almost too sacred to try to describe with mere words. This is one of those moments that gently cradles your heat-blistered face in its hands and says, "It's not about your discomfort, my sweaty friend. *THIS is the whole purpose of your presence. LOVE* conquers everything. You are here because you *LOVE* them."

God's Love is intentional and purposeful, always. It has an origination, a direction and a destination, always. Surrendering to God's intention and purpose leads to victory. Always.

God truly has created all things, all times, all events with distinct purpose and intentionality. In the previous chapter we reviewed the list of witnesses in Hebrews 11 & 12. We learned that faith in God as revealed by scripture has the intentional implication that, if one claims/takes ownership of this faith *(pistis)*, then the result is that actions based on trust in God will manifest within the believer. Further, a long-term result of this faith is a lifestyle based on this chosen belief system. Where faith is a lifestyle, attitudes are grounded in confidence. Where attitudes are grounded in confidence then hope is the mechanism through which thoughts and decisions are filtered.

God's ways are always intentional, meaning there is purpose behind His works and His design. As we begin, we are going to search for those intentions, those examples of planned purpose from God. We will also begin the process of discovery, where we

will ask God to show us new insights concerning His intentional purpose for mankind, and for each of us personally.

Bear in mind that God has already *intentionally* left us all the evidence we need for this process! It must be our intention, then, to earnestly seek revelation in order that God's direction can be wholeheartedly followed. God wishes to be sovereign over every aspect of our lives. We must continually seek new insights so there will be no remaining neglected, dark corners of ourselves that have never been surrendered. Without the continual act of surrender, transformation ceases and growth is stagnated. Therefore let us search with hope, because we confidently expect that the effort will be beneficial.

Original Design, Original Designer

> *"By faith we understand that the universe was formed at God's command, so that what is seen was not made out of what is visible." (Hebrews 11:3)*

> *"This is the account of the heavens and the earth when they were created.*
> *When the LORD God made the earth and the heavens—no shrub of the field had yet appeared on the earth and no plant of the field had yet sprung up, for the LORD had not sent rain on the earth and there was no man to work the ground, but streams came up from the earth and watered the whole surface of the ground—the LORD God formed the man from the dust of the ground and breathed into his nostrils the breath of life, and man became a living being.*
> *Now the LORD God had planted a garden in the east, in Eden; and there he put the man he had formed. And the LORD God made all kinds of trees grow out of the ground— trees that were pleasing to the eye and good for food." (Genesis 2:4-9)*

> "The LORD God took the man and put him in the Garden of Eden to work and take care of it. And the LORD God commanded the man, 'You are free to eat from any tree in the garden; but you must not eat of the tree of the knowledge of good and evil, for when you eat of it, you will surely die.' The LORD God said, 'It is not good for man to be alone. I will make a suitable helper for him.' "
>
> Now the LORD God had formed out of the ground all the beasts of the field and birds of the air. He brought them to the man to see what he would name them; and whatever the man called each living creature, that was its name. So, the man gave names to all the livestock, the birds of the air and all the beasts of the field.
>
> But for Adam no suitable helper was found. So the LORD God caused the man to fall into a deep sleep; while he was sleeping, he took one of the man's ribs and closed up the place with flesh. Then the LORD God made the woman from the rib he had taken out of the man, and he brought her to the man.
>
> The man said,
> 'This is now bone of my bones, and flesh of my flesh; She shall be called woman, for she was taken out of man.'
> For this reason a man will leave his father and mother and be united to his wife, and they will become one flesh.
> The man and his wife were naked, and they felt no shame."
> (Genesis 2:15-25)

There is an enormous feast before us in these words. The scriptures have revealed much as to God's intention and design from the beginning of mankind. Searching for a deeper understanding, researching original text and context, we can draw out some valuable nuggets of information.

First, it is important to remember that the Creator of the Universe can speak and things happen. There is nothing more God has to do beyond uttering words and it's a done deal. Why is

this noteworthy? Because this is the way God created everything that is in existence today. That is, everything except mankind.

God used His own hands to fashion man, leaving His own fingerprints on every aspect of man's being. Next, God could have merely said, "Breathe," and man would have become a living being. But God intentionally blew life into man from His own breath, His own seat of life. The root word here (*the Hebrew, "ruah"*) literally means that God gave breath to man, and by extension of the meaning created man's heart, spirit and mind – the unseen, eternal part of a person that connects and responds to God. No other being created has this. Nothing else in creation is connected to God's eternal nature. Only man bears God's own breath. Certainly other creatures have what is referred to as the breath of life, but the meaning intended there is that they became living, with breathing. And according to Genesis 1: 20-25, God said, "Let there be…" His words spoke them into existence. In Genesis 1: 26-27, God said, "Let us make…" thereby revealing His intention to purposefully use His own hands to create, rather than just speak. This singular, intentional difference should help us to understand just how precious we are to God.

Continuing, each and every living thing in creation was made with the ability to sustain itself, and the ability to reproduce. But Adam had no one. There was nothing in all creation that was precious enough for man.

Here it is especially important to pay attention. The God of all creation, who can speak things into existence and who formed man with His own hands, made a purposeful and intentional decision. He did not choose to make woman out of the dust of the ground. No, God's creation, man, was complete and perfect and holy in every way but one: he was unable to multiply, to perpetuate his kind. So our loving Father God took something out of man's completeness and fashioned woman. The root word used when referring to the creation of woman *from man* in this passage (*the Hebrew, "sela"*) literally means opposite side. This fact alone should cause some major shifts in our perceptions of male/female relationships.

God's crowning achievement in creation was man and woman. God's intentional purpose in creating them from one being is that they would complement each other. The only way for man to have a suitable companion, or suitable support, was for God to remove something of very real value and significance from man and make it His intentional design for woman. It is clear, then, that God intended that we not only acknowledge but truly embrace that which we lack, in order to receive completeness when united with our spouse. We are created to be better, stronger, and even more formidable…*together!*

Next, it is equally important to recognize that both man and woman bear the "*ruah*" of God. Both male and female, therefore, are equally precious to God. Both bear their Creator's likeness. When they were placed in the garden and entrusted with its stewardship, there began the perfect bond intended by God. Man and woman were in a unified, dependent relationship with the origin of their existence. Unity of the three is demonstrated by God's bestowing stewardship of His garden to man and woman. Dependence is demonstrated by man's reliance on God for the providence of all his needs. The three shared love, trust and purpose.

Finally, let us search to see if there is any evidence of resentment or feelings of inferiority at this time. You will be searching a long time, because there are none, yet. The original design of God's creation never mentions that the male's role is superior to that of the female. Certainly man's stature was larger and stronger than woman's. It is still that way today. Man probably did most of the heavy work, and woman probably did what was suited to her being. There also is no mention of man being particularly disgruntled because he's not the one who is designed to carry the offspring. Each was content with who they were created to be and each was content with relying on the source of all life to provide for their needs. Whatever was provided, *that was enough.*

There was no thought even conceived that might cause disunity between them.

Points to Ponder

This is precious information, friends. We could affect our surroundings with a positive force if we could align ourselves with God's original intentions. Think about it. Ask yourself:

- How far off is my attitude concerning these very things?
- Have I carried resentment towards anyone or any gender, and now that I have seen God's original intention I find that my attitude is wrong?

Perhaps it is time to take a moment of prayer and reflection. Perhaps each of us should ask God to renew our hearts to walk closely with His intentions. Breathe in, and blow out. Breathe in deeply, and know that God is with you! With every breath you take God is saying, "I will sustain you." Look in the mirror. Every detail you see is God saying, "I formed you with my own hands, and I love you… just the way you are."

His breath sustains you, and His hands formed you! God's love is intentional and purposeful. It originates with Him, moves directly to your benefit and reaches its destination when received in your being. Always.

Chapter 3
Destinations and Detours

My family, as previously stated, is precious to me. We have been known to travel great distances in order to be together. Hence, travel is also a big part of our lives. When traveling, I say flying is the way to go. There is no amount of security or scrutiny that has changed my mind as of yet. I have had the privilege of experiencing both commercial and private flight, and have enjoyed all that is available from upgraded first class to puddle hopping with chickens on the adjacent seat.

I find small aircraft particularly fascinating. This fact is never to be confused with actually desiring to personally fly small aircraft. I merely find myself marveling at those who do. There are several people in my life who are commercial pilots, as well as those who command personal and corporate planes of various sizes. As an added bonus, it is humorous to sit in on conversations with any combination of these guys, trying desperately to understand their lingo.

One such occasion involved a detailed description of flights that went tragically wrong. The discussion centered on the "attitude" of the aircraft, and how any mistake—even by one tiny degree—could be deadly.

The attitude, taking huge liberties here, refers to keeping the nose of the plane level and moving towards the intended destination. A downward attitude will eventually crash the aircraft. Equally as deadly, an upward attitude will take the plane into air that is too thin for the engine to continue working. Losing oxygen, the plane will stall. With no forward movement, gravity takes over like a rock falling off a ledge. As pilots operate their aircraft, constant attention to adjustments is required. One degree off to the right or to the left over the course of many miles, and the intended target destination is completely missed. Wind currents, weather disturbances and varying topography all force continual vigilance and adjustments to the plane's attitude. Is there any wonder they all give thanks for autopilot?

In every aspect of this example we can take lessons for how to follow God. We must be committed to keeping our attitudes in check, not aiming in any direction that could cause our spirits to be in peril. We must vigilantly attend to the direction of our hearts. We must never aim downward by underestimating the power of God. We must never aim higher than God, believing we are able to control things on our own. We must always aim purposefully *towards God* in all things.

Trouble in Paradise

Thus man and woman were in a unified, dependent relationship with God. As we will see, however, not all is peaceful in paradise. The serpent is about to enter the picture, and we will study the results of altering God's design, even to a small degree. For as much as God's intentional design is unity and dependence, Satan's intentions are to cause division and the delusion of self-sufficiency. We will also see in Genesis, chapter 4, that one act of sin, or one commitment to righteousness, can change the entire course of a family for generations to come.

"Now the serpent was more crafty than any of the animals the LORD God had made. He said to the woman, "Did God really say, 'You must not eat fruit from any tree in the garden'?"
The woman said to the serpent, 'We may eat from the trees in the garden, but God did say, 'You must not eat fruit from the tree that is in the middle of the garden, and you must not touch it, or you will die'.'
'You will not surely die,' the serpent said to the woman. 'For God knows when you eat of it your eyes will be opened, and you will be like God, knowing good and evil.' When the woman saw that the fruit of the tree was good for food and pleasing to the eye, and also desirable for gaining wisdom, she took some and ate it. She also gave some to her husband who was with her, and he ate it. Then the eyes of both of them were opened, and they realized they were naked; so they sewed fig leaves together and made coverings for themselves.
Then the man and his wife heard the sound of the LORD God walking in the garden in the cool of the day, and they hid from the LORD God among the trees of the garden. But the LORD God called to the man, 'Where are you?'
He answered, ' I heard you in the garden, and I was afraid because I was naked.'
And he said, 'Who told you were naked? Have you eaten from the tree that I commanded you not to eat from?'
The man said, 'The woman you put here with me—she gave me some fruit from the tree and I ate it.'
Then the LORD God said to the woman, 'What is this you have done?'
'The serpent deceived me, and I ate.'
So the LORD God said to the serpent,
'Because you have done this, cursed are you above all the livestock and all the wild animals! You will crawl on your belly and you will eat dust from the ground all the days of your life. And I will put enmity between you and the woman, and between your offspring and hers; he will crush your head, and you will strike his heel.'

To the woman he said,
'I will greatly increase your pains in childbearing; with pain you will give birth to children. Your desire will be for your husband, and he will rule over you.'
To Adam he said,
*'Because you listened to your wife and ate from the tree about which I commanded you 'You must not eat',
Cursed is the ground because of you; through painful toil you will eat of it all the days of your life. It will produce thorns and thistles for you, and you will eat the plants of the field. By the sweat of your brow you will eat your food until you return to the ground, since from it you were taken; for dust you are and to dust you will return.'
Adam named his wife Eve because she would become the mother of all living.
The LORD God made garments of skin for Adam and his wife and clothed them.
And the LORD God said,
'The man has now become like one of us, knowing good and evil. He must not be allowed to reach out his hand and take also from the tree of life and eat, and live forever.'
So, the LORD God banished him from the Garden of Eden to work the ground from which he had been taken. After he drove the man out, he placed on the east side of the Garden of Eden a cherubim and a flaming sword flashing back and forth to guard the way to the tree of life." (Genesis 3:1- 24)*

One Degree

It is clear that Adam and Eve met with something that caused them to veer off course. Satan knows precisely where to attack, in the most vulnerable places, in order to accomplish his intentions. Are we at all surprised he begins with a subtle attack on the confidence of the woman?

By asking her if she is sure about what has been asked of her, he causes doubt within her. Her response, overstating what

God's command was (for God never said not to touch the tree) shows that she is willing to alter the actual truth, just one degree. Next Satan uses a half-truth of his own (you will not surely die; you will be like God) to nudge her off course further. Her focus is no longer on obeying God, but on her own dwindling grasp of trusting who God created her to be, and she is starting to lose sight that God sufficiently provides for her every need.

The words used in the original text show that Satan appeals to her by saying if she will eat the fruit, she will come to recognize things the way her Creator does, and that she will successfully have wisdom and power as well as a potent capacity to understand and exercise skill the same way God does. The seeds of disobedience have now been planted in the soil of ego. As they sprout and take root, she looks at the beautiful fruit before her. She now gives way to coveting the fruit for what she thinks it will bring her—wisdom equal to God's—and then explains away her corrupt frame of mind by rationalizing that it is good for food. (You have to love how God just explained the whole root of every problem with women. Irrational Rationalizing.)

Before we jump on the fault bandwagon, let's remember that the man is equally to blame. The scripture clearly states that he was with her. He was standing right there, watching the whole thing play out. He has full knowledge that what his wife is about to do is against God's command. Man has been working this garden from the very beginning and knows there is absolutely no need for any more "good food," as their needs are completely supplied. When she gives him that which is forbidden and he finally has the opportunity to do what is right in the sight of God... he completely caves in to the pretty face. (You have to love how God just explained the whole root of every problem with men. Physical Vision vs. Spiritual Vision)

Herein lies the point that must be meditated upon. God, by His very nature, being creator of all things and the origination of all life, knows the full intricacies of all that is good and evil. He IS divine completeness and therefore knows all things.

For man, who is human in form and intellect, the knowledge of good and evil manifests in an extremely limited capacity. We cannot *see* all things, nor can we *foreknow* anything. We are limited to the vision of "now," and therefore can't fully comprehend the long-term, far-reaching effects of disobedient decisions. Therefore it is both dangerous and frightening to step even one degree away from God's design. When we do, it is to our own peril.

The Birth of Sin

In one act, Satan has succeeded in bringing pride and disobedience into the world. Where there once was purity in man's relationship with God there is now broken trust. Where there was once dependence on God, there now is the birth of selfishness and the illusion of self-reliance. The sins of both Adam and Eve were committed because their attitudes weren't corrected to stay on course.

The price to be paid is steep. Where there was unity, the punishment is separation, and the emptiness and longing that accompany the now broken God-Man relationship. Further, Satan has successfully corrupted the purity of the Man-Woman relationship as created by God. Where there once were attitudes of harmony and the appreciation for the strengths and differences created in each other, there are now downward attitudes of resentment and blame. Now, throughout the ages, all mankind will avoid accountability by using blame.

For every relationship between man and woman until the end of time, there will always be something imperfect. No matter how strongly she is drawn towards man, there will always be a small remaining thread of woman's attitude that aims to be higher, that is willing to manipulate him to get her way, and in its harshest extreme wishes to use her desirable form to control him. And no matter how he feels about woman, there will always be a small remaining thread of man's attitude that aims lower, that withholds his trust from that which is distinctly female, and in

its harshest form wishes to punish her by using her own need for acceptance against her. As sad as this reality is, look around you. The power struggle is still in play today. We must attend vigilantly to our attitudes, leveling often, if we wish to stay on course with God's pattern for our relationships.

The Weight of Punishment

Most noteworthy, now, are God's actions in the face of fallen man. The God who is the seat of life and creator of all things could have started over again. God could have struck man and woman dead. He certainly had the power to do so. He didn't. Although He banished them from the garden, thereby changing the course of the lives of all mankind, He also spoke immediately of the way that all mankind would be brought back to Him. He spoke of the one to come, Jesus.

> *"I will put enmity between you and the woman, and between your offspring and hers; he will crush your head, and you will strike his heel." (Genesis 3:15)*

In this powerful statement, God invoked punishment to Satan, the serpent, by condemning him to crawl on his belly, but that isn't all. God looked Satan squarely in the eye and said, "You may have won this battle, but you will lose the war. I AM GOD. I am all-powerful, and there is one who is coming. The one who is coming through this woman's descendants will deal you your final blow, and you will lose. You might inflict harm to my mankind, but your harm is merely a sad little flesh wound. There is one who will overcome. I AM GOD."

The punishment for Adam and Eve isn't nearly as severe, but completely appropriate. Neither one of them respected God's authority over them. Neither one of them valued the "completeness" of who they were together. Prior to this moment, man easily sustained himself from the plenty found in Eden.

Prior to this moment, his only accountability was himself. Now he will have to leave the ease and plenty of the garden and work hard. Now he will have the burden and responsibility of taking care of woman. While there is a portion of our population that believes that being "boss" over woman is their right, God is clear. Man will be judged on how he governs. Man failed to protect the woman from corruption in the garden. Failure to protect her from what is corrupt and in opposition to God's way now will only reap continued judgment.

Woman's punishment is not to be confused either. Because she tried not only to assert herself above man, but also tried to become equal with God, she is now in a position that requires that she respect that which God's authority has placed in man's care: herself. Because she failed to recognize how precious she is to God and questioned her value, she will always be tied to how much man values her.

Also in the face of sadness, God chose to ultimately bless. Although man would have to toil for his sustenance, the ground would still bear him food. Although giving birth would be toilsome and painful, Eve was still allowed to be what she was created to be, the Mother of All. God reassured them through his message of the one who would crush Satan's head, that they were still loved, still so precious in fact that Satan will be completely destroyed for what harm he has done.

Finally, God provides clothing for His children. The leaves they had sewn were insufficient for them outside of the garden environment. God made durable clothing out of animal skins that would properly protect them from the elements. Once again, here is the example that no matter how hard we try to rely on ourselves for what we need, it is completely insufficient. Only God can give us precisely what we need, exactly when we need it.

Points to Ponder

As you meditate on all we've examined, there is much to be considered.

- How is your understanding of the God-Man relationship changing?
- How is your perception of the Man-Woman relationship changing?
- In light of acknowledging the limitations of our humanness, where are the areas of your life in which your attitudes need to be corrected and set back on course with God?
- What are some specific current cultural influences that can adversely affect God's design for these relationships?

Chapter 4
Changing Course

One recent trip to New York City was for the purpose of settling my daughter into her new apartment. Having recently graduated with a shiny new journalism degree and currently waiting tables while trying to land a job with a national magazine, her furnishings were Spartan at best. Another reason for the trip was to reunite her with her little doggie companion who had been staying with us until she could rent an appropriate flat. An appropriate flat in the safest area in the Upper East Side is pricey to say the least. With every penny spoken for, our nose to the grindstone girl needed the homey comforts that only a Mother's love and credit card could provide.

We literally ran ourselves ragged lifting boxes, assembling furniture and teaching puppy how to be a good little city dog who uses a leash at all times and makes nice with the dog park crowd. The sheer size of Manhattan and the lack of a car made for long days and navigational nightmares. We managed to treat ourselves to a few decent meals and more than a couple of amazing bagels, but for the most part we were all business.

The one exception, per my request, was our side trip to Ellis Island. Having lost my Dad just two months before, I had gone through his safety deposit box sorting documents and papers. To my surprise, I found the original immigration papers for my Mother's Dad who was originally from Scotland. The delight was bittersweet for my brother and me. Our Mom obviously strategically placed these papers for our discovery at a time when she could still make crucial decisions, before she drifted away from us to Alzheimer's disease. As she is the last surviving sibling, there is no one remaining to fill in the details of this part of our family history. There is, however, the American Family Immigration History Center on Ellis Island.

If you haven't already done so, a visit to Ellis Island should be on everyone's to-do list. The ferry ride to the island includes a stop to see the Statue of Liberty. The view of Manhattan is gorgeous, especially at sunset when the colors reflect off of the towering glass metropolis.

We arrived late in the day, and in January, which meant we almost had the place to ourselves. We spent a bit of time looking at the displays and pictures, but I was anxious to get to the computers. The staff at the History Center is enormously helpful, and genuinely excited when one finds a connection to someone who passed through these halls. As the last visitors of the day, we had their full attention.

My daughter and I entered the limited information I had into the database and waited for a response. Immediately the images of a ship's log and signatures of passengers flashed on the screen. There, five rows down from the top, was my grandfather's signature, his age, his hometown and his port of departure. We saw amazing pictures of the ship that brought him here, steerage class of course. Scrolling over we saw his occupation: "Confectioner." That's right, my Grandpa was a candy maker. There was the name of the ship, and the day he arrived, and the name of the friend with whom he'd be staying. And the address… in America!

What happened next was the icing on the cake. The women in the History Center excitedly looked at us and asked, "Would you like to see where he came in?" We were out of our seats in a

flurry; I don't think we even answered. They walked us into the main hall, the one you see in all the pictures with the beautifully tiled ceiling and the windows looking out at Lady Liberty. They walked me to the middle of the floor and said, "Every person who came through this immigration center, until 1924, came through this very room."

Their words echoed; we were the only people there except three men huddled on a bench making plans for a movie here. I could scarcely take it all in. It was dumbfounding. Hundreds of thousands came through here with little more than the clothes on their backs, all in search of a better life for their families. My grandfather was one of them. As we exited, I was asked if my grandfather stayed in Manhattan or immediately left for another city. "According to the records," I answered, "he stayed here." They immediately moved us to the very staircase where my grandfather would have walked to enter his new life. These stairs are the only part of Ellis Island that have never been updated or refurbished. These literally are the exact stairs he descended.

I lost it. I lost all composure and blubbered like a baby. I'm not even sure why, but I couldn't stop the floodgates. My hosts assured me that this is a very common occurrence, and especially at this location, but even that didn't help my astonishment at my reaction.

On the ferry ride back it finally hit me. This is the place where my grandfather changed the course of our family forever. This one decision had far reaching implications, and set the direction for my life as well. Had he not come to America, my Mother would have been born in Scotland. Had she been born in Scotland, she would have married there as well, never meeting my Dad. Had she never met and married my Dad, I would have been adoptively placed in a completely different family; I would likely have never met my husband, and never had the children we have, including the daughter standing next to me on that boat. One decision changed everything.

As we continue following our spiritual family history, we will also see how one decision can forever change the course of those who will follow.

The Decision

Adam lay with his wife Eve, and she became pregnant and gave birth to Cain. She said, "With the help of the LORD I have brought forth a man." Later she gave birth to his brother Abel.

Now Abel kept flocks and Cain worked the soil. In the course of time Cain brought some of the fruits of the soil as an offering to the LORD. But Abel brought fat portions from some of the firstborn of his flock. The LORD looked with favor on Abel and his offering, but on Cain and his offering he did not look with favor. So Cain was very angry and his face was downcast.

The LORD said to Cain, "Why is your face downcast? If you do what is right, will you not be accepted? But if you do not do what is right, sin is crouching at your door; it desires to have you, but you must master it."

Now Cain said to his brother Abel, "Lets go out to the field." And while they were in the field, Cain attacked his brother Abel and killed him.

Then the LORD said to Cain, "Where is your brother Abel?" "I don't know," he replied. "Am I my brother's keeper?"

The LORD said, "What have you done? Listen! Your brother's blood cries out to me from the ground. Now you are under a curse and driven from the ground, which opened its mouth to receive your brother's blood from your hand. When you work the ground, it will no longer yield crops for you. You will be a restless wanderer on the earth."

Cain said to the LORD, "My punishment is more than I can bear. Today you are driving me from the land, and I will be hidden from your presence; I will be a restless wanderer on the earth, and whoever finds me will kill me."

But the LORD said to him, "Not so; if anyone kills Cain, he will suffer vengeance seven times over." Then the LORD put a mark on Cain so that no one who found him would kill him. So Cain went out from the LORD'S presence, and lived in the land of nod, east of Eden. (Genesis 4:1-16)

Adam and Eve, no longer having access to the garden, are living in the area of Eden working the ground from which he had been taken. They have two sons, first Cain, and then Abel. The older son joins his father in working the land, while his younger brother takes the job of tending the animals. All of this begs the question, as Adam and Eve are now imperfect because of sin, how have their imperfections affected their offspring's view of the LORD and the world? In the story we've read we have our answers.

It is clear that these sons have been taught that one should serve the LORD and acknowledge Him as their creator and source of all sustenance. It also becomes clear that the sons have very different attitudes on who God is (God-Man Relationship) and how God should be honored. Cain is willing to go through the motions of sacrifice, but gives little thought to what would be acceptable. Abel, on the other hand, makes a thoughtful choice to offer the best from what he has been given as an acknowledgement of The One from whom it came.

There is an opportunity for Cain to course correct, but in the end his choice leaves sin to having dominion over him rather than the opposite, and he murders his brother, his ill-perceived rival for God's affections.

It is noteworthy to see that when referring to man "ruling" over woman, and Cain needing to "master" the sin crouching at his door, the same Hebrew word is used. The word, *masal*, literally refers to governing control and dominion. God is saying to Cain, just as He did to Adam concerning his wife, "This is your responsibility and it's in your jurisdiction buddy, so handle it. It's up to you to point it in the direction it should go."

The Trajectory

Sadly, Cain's choice changes his direction forever. He is sent away from his parents and his LORD. Because his sin soaked the ground, the source of all mankind and the source of his life's sustenance, with the life-blood of his brother, the ground would now cease to sustain him. Cain's objective cries weren't very sincere either. His only concern was the effect banishment would have on *him*, not that he had done wrong, or that his action caused grief to his parents. He was still missing the attitude adjustment that would bring him back into alignment with God. The sin of pride, born out of Adam and Eve's poor choices, is now manifesting in larger stature within their son. The fallout not only leaves them without Abel, it takes Cain from them as well. This second degree off from God's design now sets a new trajectory for those who will follow. Let's look at the results.

(Outlined in Genesis 4:17- 5: 24)

Trajectory of SIN   *Trajectory of RIGHTEOUSNESS*

ADAM

Trajectory of SIN	Trajectory of RIGHTEOUSNESS
Cain	Seth
Enoch	Enosh
Irad	Kenan
Mehujael	Mahalalel
Methushael	Jared
Lamech	Enoch

(then Methuselah- Lamech- Noah)

*To the seventh generation from Adam through Cain , was Lamech. Lamech's pride, arrogance and selfishness/self-reliance are summed up in his declaration in Genesis 4:23 & 24. He dares to lay personal claim to God's pronouncement of protection for Cain, and the vengeance that would result should someone seek their own justice. Moreover, he arrogantly boasts of murdering

someone who crossed him. The sins were in their infancy when born through Cain but have reached fully grown stature in Lamech. (Who also brought polygamy into the world.)

Conversely, as shown in Gen 4:26, Adam's line through Seth began to *"call on the name of the LORD."* It becomes clear that Adam and Eve do not want to make the same mistakes with Seth that took their other two sons from them. By correcting their attitude and teaching their son how to stay on course with God, Seth's descendants continued to reflect this lifestyle. Keeping their attitudes aligned with God, they seek to serve Him in righteousness. Fast-forward to the seventh generation (Hebrews 11: 5-6, Genesis 5:21-24) and righteousness has reached its full stature in Enoch. According to scripture he did not experience death. He was *"taken away"* because it is noted, *"he walked with God."* This is the family line through which God accomplishes His will on the earth.

Points to Ponder
Staying on Course

In the following reading, reflect on the preciousness of these words.

But as for me, I will always have hope;
I will praise you more and more.
My mouth will tell of your righteousness,
of your salvation all day long,
though I know not its measure.
I will come and proclaim your mighty acts,
O Sovereign LORD;
I will proclaim your righteousness,
yours alone.
Since my youth, O God,
you have taught me, and to this day
I declare your marvelous deeds.

> *Even when I am old and gray,*
> *do not forsake me, O God,*
> *till I declare your power to the next generation,*
> *your might to all who are to come.*
> *(Psalm 71: 14-18)*

- How can God use these words to fill your heart with hope?
- In which areas of your life can you use these words to keep your focus on God?
- Where do you need to adjust your attitude, or your trajectory, in order to be aligned correctly with God?
- Who has God placed within your jurisdiction—your scope of influence—that will benefit from discovering God's direction for their life?

Ask God to use these words to fill your heart with hope, and keep your focus on Him. Spend some time in prayer asking God to show you where you need to adjust your attitude, your trajectory, in order to show His direction to those who come after you.

Chapter 5

The Rainbow... After The Rain

There are moments in life when you realize your existence has been altered permanently. Those moments arrive neither graciously nor politely; they do, however, demand your gracious and polite adjustment. The inevitable timing of such moments, it seems, is excruciating, embarrassing, unexpected, and, naturally, public. By way of explanation, our family reunion time as we gathered for the Maryland wedding was not only very exciting and happy for us; it was also, in varying degrees, difficult as well. In a sense, it was like the rainbow...after the storm.

The initial arrival to my cousin's home last summer was the absolute best way to begin. Carefully strategized, this introductory hug-fest eased us into the eventual pangs of sadness. Each of us had, in a spiritual sense, arrived in much the same way one dashes into shelter breathlessly after getting unexpectedly caught in a torrential downpour, sans umbrella. Although you find yourself relieved and thankful to be out of the storm, you eventually have to deal with your soaked-to-the-skin clothing.

The Rain

When I described us as a conglomeration of a hot mess, this was no exaggeration. The years between our visits have been filled with what can only be termed "Real Life." Our family has, as a whole, faced torrential downpours of challenges.

The enthusiasm with which we looked forward to gathering for some collective healing cannot be overstated. Like a fleet of ships heading home after riding out a hurricane, we were all purposefully navigating to this safe harbor. Each of us brought much happiness, looking towards the future. The happiness, however, arrived toting some steamer trunk-size baggage from the unresolved trauma of past storms. Heavy as my personal baggage can be, I was bound to drop it at some point, and that point came at The Farm.

Immediately upon entering my Aunt's home at The Farm, scents from the kitchen filled the air. Again, many favorites covered the kitchen counters and we, being raised to be the polite southerners we are, dove into the appetizers with abandon. Sweet and savory flavors dancing in my mouth, I should have been prepared for the parallel. There, amid the laughing, stories, picture posing and shrimp dip came the sucker punch. As I reached for my drink on the buffet, my parents' broad smiles landed right on my heart. They weren't there, you see. It was their photograph. It was a picture of laughing smiles and a happier time. This was the first full family gathering in my fifty years of living where they weren't present.

Don't let anyone fool you into thinking you can ever be prepared to lose a parent. Every life is divided into two existences: with parents and without. No matter how long you have to adjust to the idea, when it happens you are most definitely not ready. Also, there is a tricky little companion named Grief. There is no front desk for this life stage to check in and check out, and it arrives without the courtesy of reservations. Mr. Grief took up residence with me when we lost Dad six months earlier, just before

Thanksgiving after a prolonged hospital stay. Mrs. Grief has been here a while, since we lost Mom too, but not to death. Several years ago, Alzheimer's claimed the precious lady we used to know, leaving a very pleasant gal we visit frequently and a gaping hole in the family landscape.

There were others' holes, of course, each one named after one of the many trials the family has experienced in the past few years. The not-so-funny thing about holes is if you're not careful in your navigation, you'll most likely fall right in. The race course for the weekend, it seemed, was now set. We would spend the remainder of our reunion-run helping each other past our personal pitfalls. At that very moment, however, I felt myself sprawling headlong. Were it not for the timely rescue from my cousin's daughter, I could have completely embarrassed myself. With a gigantic hug from Lexa, and a deeply sincere, "I'm so glad you're here," I quietly lifted my glass towards Mom and Dad—towards the life I once knew and the life I now face without them—composed myself and moved on.

The Prayer Post

The Farm came into the family relatively recently. My Aunt and Uncle, loving the charm and history of the property, purchased it as a true fixer-upper upon my Uncle's retirement from education. Having been a high school principal for decades, he knows how to run things. Love, imagination and raw sweat turned this long neglected place into a real beauty.

The house is colonial-genteel, with low ceilings and creaky stairs, and the newer addition of a large family room that can hold a crowd. Many of our families' memories took shape in this room. Countless photographs line every imaginable surface, recalling dates and events of every historical significance to our family tree. This particular room has a massive picture window that reveals the rear pastures of the property, home to the horses. They are part of the family, too, but are deeply connected to my Uncle. The minute he emerges from the door, they whinny for him in full chorus. The horses know *exactly* who takes care of them.

Every day my Uncle attends to the needs of his family, and to the various animals in residence here. In just over eighty years, I don't think there has ever been a time when he wasn't caring for someone. I treasure every time I get to accompany him to the barn, my hand held firmly in his protective grasp. We greet the horses, feed the cats, brush a mane or two, and mostly just enjoy the company. The walk back to the house is never direct. The one regularly scheduled stop is mid-way back, at the Prayer Post.

The Prayer Post is a very special place for our family. It is a place to stop and remember. It is a place to look closely at our past, receiving and embracing its lessons so as to reach confidently into the future. It is here where prayers have been lifted on behalf of each person loved and treasured. Here, thanksgiving and praise have been offered. My Uncle is certain this is the best place to pray. There are no cell towers, no buildings, no trees; just a direct call line to the Heavenly Father. My Uncle knows *exactly* who takes care of him.

To be fair, our family's recent burdens could have easily ruined the intentional purpose of the weekend, but this spot alone is what held us through everything. This is where God was asked to bless the upcoming nuptials. This is where God was asked to guard our travels and bring us safely together. This is where God was asked to bind our hearts in strength and unity as we collectively put so much "on hold" for a period of celebration: the wounds inflicted by a cheating husband, the pain of facing alcoholism, the frustration of struggling businesses in a devastated economy, the sadness of dealing with Alzheimer's disease, the deep grief of loss. Here God was asked to "fix" amid that which is unfixable. This is where God was asked to heal our hearts as we celebrated the first major family event without my Dad, without my Mom, without beloved Grandparents. This, above all, is where we took time to acknowledge that God reaches down to each of us and simply blesses.

My Uncle is a very wise man. He has seen both the beauty and ugliness that comes with real life. He has celebrated the blessings when there is smooth sailing. He has seen the damage when things go terribly wrong. The one thing he has taught me that will forever hold true is this: When things go wrong, going back to God is always right.

Noah, Before & After

As we continue examining the *Faith of the Ancients* as outlined throughout Hebrews, chapters 11 & 12, we will see a pattern. God shows us consistently that the path of those who obey Him leaves a trail of conclusive evidence. Over and over again we see that obedient actions bring honor and glory to Him. We also see that God honors those who are obedient with protection and blessing. Throughout time, faith was demonstrated within the context of choices rooted in trust and confidence in God, who has the power to provide all things. Those who willfully sought their own direction, under the influence of selfishness, pride, arrogance and disobedience, found that their direction ended in their ruination—even their complete destruction.

In Genesis, chapters 8 & 9, we find Noah and his family emerging from the great rain and flood into a new life. The old life is completely gone, destroyed in the floodwaters. As he exits the ark, which was their protection from destruction, he stops with his family and builds an altar to God to remember who has taken care of them. Here is where they offer sacrifice of thanksgiving and where God chooses to bless them as they move forward into their life—after the rain.

But what brought them to this place? What were the events of their lives that left them here on unfamiliar ground, acknowledging things of the past yet moving forward with gratitude? To understand how Noah is facing the future, we must look closely at his past, receiving and embracing the lessons that will give us confidence and hope—hope that will sustain us even in our own storms and floods.

Our answers are in the previous chapters of Genesis. Here we see mankind has multiplied and greatly populated the earth. The descendants of Cain and the descendants of Seth inhabit the same general territories. The full effects of rebelliousness can be seen at every turn. God is overwhelmed with a deep grief and makes a drastic decision.

> "When Lamech had lived 182 years, he had a son. He named him Noah and said, 'He will comfort us in the labor and painful toil of our hands caused by the ground the LORD has cursed.' After Noah was born, Lamech lived 595 years and had other sons and daughters. Altogether Lamech lived 777 years, and then he died.
> After Noah was 500 years old, he became the father of Shem, Ham and Japheth.
> When men began to increase in number on the earth and daughters were born to them, the sons of God saw that the daughters of men were beautiful, and they married any of them they chose. Then the LORD said, 'My spirit will not contend with man forever, for he is mortal; his days will be a hundred and twenty years.
> The Nephilim were on the earth in those days—and also afterward—when the sons of God went to the daughters of men and had children with them. They were heroes of old, men of renown.
> The LORD saw how great man's wickedness on the earth had become, and that every inclination of the thoughts of his heart was on evil all the time.
> The LORD was grieved that he had made man on the earth, and his heart was filled with pain. So the LORD said, 'I will wipe mankind, whom I have created, from the face of the earth—men and animals, and creatures that move along the ground, and birds of the air— for I am grieved that I have made them. But Noah found favor in the eyes of the LORD.
> This is the account of Noah.

Noah was a righteous man, blameless among the people of his time, and he walked with God. Noah had three sons, Shem, Ham and Japheth.
Now the earth was corrupt in God's sight and was full of violence. God saw how corrupt the earth had become, for all the people had corrupted their ways. So God said to Noah, 'I am going to put an end to all people, for the earth is filled with violence because of them. I am surely going to destroy both them and the earth. So make yourself an ark of cypress wood; make rooms in it and coat it with pitch inside and out.
This is how you are to build it: The ark is to be 450 feet long, 75 feet wide, and 45 feet high. Make a roof for it and finish the arc to within 18 inches of the top. Put a door in the side of the ark, and make lower middle and upper decks. I am going to bring floodwaters on the earth to destroy all life under the heavens, every creature that has the breath of life in it. Everything on earth will perish. But I will establish my covenant with you, and you will enter the ark—you and your sons and your wife and your sons' wives with you. You are to bring into the ark two of all living creatures, male and female, to keep them alive with you. Two of every kind of bird, of every kind of animal and every kind of animal that moves along the ground will come to you to be kept alive. You are to take every kind of food that is to be eaten and store it away as food for you and for them'
Noah did everything just as God commanded him."
(Genesis 5:28- 6:22)

My, how times have changed. Let's remember that in Genesis 1:31, God looked at creation of man and called it, *"very good."* But when we look at the literal translation of this passage in Genesis, chapters 5&6, we find that God is so distressed by how far mankind has wandered from His perfect design that He now has changed his mind about creating them. He no longer views His perfectly created world as *very good*. He views it as ruined. (Hebrew: *sahat*) He has seen the evidence that mankind's character/disposition is directed toward only violence and destruction—with intent to lay waste. (Hebrew: *hamas*)

God certainly has the capacity to completely destroy all things. However, Noah has captured God's attention. He is one who travels with God; he has found favor with God. God decides, therefore, to save Noah and his family. He commands Noah to build an ark.

What is so unusual about this command? It should be understood that the region where Noah lives is landlocked. There is no access to any large bodies of water. Also, the length of time it would take to build this vessel is not short. It is going to take years—many, many years. The account says, though, that Noah did everything, just as God commanded him.

At first examination I am humbled that Noah would have no qualms about subjecting himself to the consternation of his community as he undertakes this project. I can't even imagine the gossip about this strange family. As I meditate further, though, I realize that Noah is already drastically different from those who surround him. He remains faithful to God in an environment of complete corruption. His family is likely accustomed to being snubbed, even persecuted to some degree, because of how drastically different they are.

I have also acquired a deep respect for Noah's wife. It is one thing to be informed by one's husband that the world as you know it is coming to an end and he is going to build a gigantic boat in the back yard inside which they will find salvation. It's quite another thing to accept sharing one's nautical living quarters with animals, birds, and *things that creep along the ground.* Seriously, chew on that information for a few minutes. For years I have barely tolerated the world's least affectionate feline for the sole purpose of ridding our home of the occasional small lizard, to which I have an extreme aversion. That's just one little pet, not a full cargo of predatory cats with man-eating tendencies, not to mention the rest of their jungle friends. This woman is a saint! Her compliance and that of Noah's sons is nothing short of remarkable.

Noah's complete obedience results in two vital points. First, he and his family will have life—a completely new and uncertain future for sure, but they will be allowed to live and move forward just the same. Second, God has established a covenant promise between Noah and himself, which will be extended to Noah's descendants as well. The covenant becomes effective when Noah and his family literally leave their previous life to be buried in death in the depths of the waters, and emerge from the waters into a new life, which they dedicate to the God who takes care of them.

This is the first recorded instance in which God uses water to accomplish a means to salvation. The waters of the flood, covering the earth by rain and by the springs of the deep bursting, became the cause of death for those living in opposition to God's design—those who did not heed the call to go to the place that would save them (the ark). The waters also became the source of salvation for those living in obedience to God—those who entered the ark. The actions of Noah and his family were a confirmation—a pledge, if you will—of their trust in God. Here is one event, with two different courses of action by those who were present, and two drastically different results: Salvation for one, and destruction for the other.

Points to Ponder

Can you think of any other examples in scripture in which water is used as a source of salvation? In 1 Peter 3:18-22, it states:

> *"For Christ died for sins once for all, the righteous for the unrighteous, to bring you to God. He was put to death in the body but made alive by the Spirit, through whom also he went and preached to the spirits in prison who disobeyed long ago when God waited patiently in the days of Noah while the ark was being built. In it only a few people, eight in all, were*

> saved through water, and this water symbolizes baptism that now saves you also—not the removal of dirt from the body but the pledge (an affirmation of trust in who God is) of a good conscience toward God. It saves you by the resurrection of Jesus Christ, who has gone to heaven and is at God's right hand—with angels, authorities and powers in submission to him"

There is a definite (intentional) parallel between the example of the flood and obedience to the gospel of Christ, and it is clear that God has a design for us concerning obedience. As we begin to mature, and as we experience all that real life has in store for us, it becomes plain that there are times when we fail to be obedient children of God. No one is 100 percent obedient, 100 percent of the time. It is our failures, then, that lead us to confront those facets of ourselves where we hang onto our own ways. Whether it is inexperience, stubbornness, fearfulness or full-blown rebellion, there remains in each of us, to varying degrees, some form of disobedience.

God desires *all* of us. His will for us is perfect, and His timing is infallible. It is time, then, for us to examine our fears and our lack of trust within our faith.

- If FAITH is defined as a belief or trust with an express implication that actions based on these will follow, then where do our actions betray us?

In which situations have you failed to act faithfully due to:
- A) Inexperience? (I have never faced this situation before so I'm not sure how to act)
- B) Stubbornness? (I am quite comfortable right where I am and change just isn't allowed on my agenda right now, thank you very much)
- C) Fearfulness? (I know what I need to do, but the unknown aspects of the change that needs to happen hit my "Worry" button)

- D) Rebellion? (I know for sure what God's will is, but my actions show that I am *absolutely committed* to *not* addressing the situation)

It is difficult but essential to face those aspects of ourselves in which there is an unwillingness to completely obey the God who loves us so dearly, the God who has opened the entryway to a place of salvation. By opening our hearts to this process we additionally open ourselves to growth.

In the following there are several scriptures for personal study and reflection. Take some time to read them and meditate on the impact these words should have on our behaviors. Let the words resonate within your spirit. Take time often to pray for God to open your heart to recognize the areas in which you have not trusted Him enough to wholeheartedly obey His teachings.

May God bless you as you seek to grow in love and obedience in your walk with Him, because when things are going wrong, going back to God is always right!

SCRIPTURES FOR REVIEW
John 14:15-21
1 Peter 1:14
Ephesians 4:17- 5:12
Ephesians 5:13- 6:9
Hebrews 13: 15-17, 1 John 2:1-6

Chapter 6

Leaving Home

My family was fairly typical of my generation — two parents, two kids, a dog and grandparents close by. Every family celebration I can remember was hosted in our dining room, at the same table. Menus were consistent: meatloaf for Dad's birthday, turkey for Thanksgiving and Christmas, ham for Easter, spaghetti for my own birthday. I spent my entire youth growing up in the same house until I left for college, and only permanently changed residence upon marrying.

My husband was accustomed to geographic relocations. As a consummate Navy Brat, he lived all over the United States, as well as a few years in the Philippines. Celebratory menus were consistent even if addresses weren't. He insists (and I can confirm) that his mother's pot roast is amazing no matter where it is served, and thanks to Tupperware, her chocolate chip cookies can be enjoyed even while driving.

Our own children are Corporate Brats, which mostly impacted our two older sons who lived through a total of nine moves in a ten-year time span. They have had to leave home many times, and leaving home for college was a smooth transition for them.

Laura Ann Day

Our twin daughters took their place in our family late in the corporate game and enjoyed an uncharacteristically long stay in one residence, fifteen years to be exact. To them, that place *was* home. Every significant event was experienced within the walls of our Orlando house. Their transition to college was slightly bumpier, but all in all they were troupers. But, when the time came for them to travel to Florence, Italy, for a college semester abroad, they left our home in the wake of a permanent, life-altering transition. Within a scant three weeks of time, they were forced to face leaving those roots permanently.

My husband had recently learned that we were being transferred, and hence, moving to a new city. Our house sold in a mere ten days, contractually binding us to be out in another ten days. Our girls were scheduled to leave in the middle of this. I could barely hold it together when they stood for one last picture at our front door as we headed to the airport, striking the exact same pose as they had on the first day of school from kindergarten all the way through graduation.

On the way to the airport we tried to chat of how we would see them in just a few short weeks and how exciting traveling Europe with them would be at the completion of their studies. Our feigned enthusiasm narrowly veiled our emotions at their departure. We all avoided the reality that they were not returning to this house, their home, ever again. I can close my eyes, even now, and see them vanishing into the crowd at the terminal, knowing they were fighting the urge to turn and wave because doing so would result in a flood of tears—theirs and ours.

Everyone who is a parent knows how that vision haunted us the entire time they were gone. Oh, how we prayed they would be able to put the move behind them and embrace their experience in Italy. Our prayer was answered later that summer, when we finally met our girls in Florence. As we waited in the crowds milling about on the steps of Santa Maria del Fiore, we spotted them. Confidently striding through the square, sporting Italian sunglasses and fashion, they broke into a full run, arms open,

just as thrilled to see us as we were to see them. Our reunion was joyful, and we could barely take in all the stories they shared of their studies, travels and new friends over dinner that evening.

What an astonishing transition! When they walked into that airport terminal just a few short weeks before, they were still, in our hearts at least, very much our little girls. Hadn't we—just yesterday it seemed—been sharing stories over french fries and kid's meals? Here we were, basking in the glow of candlelight, incredible Italian cuisine, and the experiences of refined young adults. It was clear that after leaving home behind, our daughters had truly opened themselves to their future and were becoming amazing and accomplished women.

Bye-Bye Chicken Nuggets

As we continue to feast at the banquet table of our spiritual ancestors, we come to what I will call some real meat. Many of the previous stories could be classified as light, easy to chew and easy to digest—spiritual *Happy Meals* of sorts; nuggets with fries on the side. Now, however, is the time to leave the kids' table behind. A place has been set for us to feast on grown-up fare indeed, the story of Abraham. This life story is going to require time and effort. Like a perfectly prepared filet mignon, there is so much more to what is being served to us in the scripture reference than meets the eye. There is a considerable process by which a 1500-pound Angus cow is refined into a delectable 8 ounces of pure perfection. In parallel, I suggest we take time to reflect and appreciate how this great follower of Yahweh left the bulk of that which defined him behind, allowing God to skillfully trim away everything that was inconsistent with the man He was refining Abraham to be, and the purpose to be fulfilled through his life.

After the Flood

As we follow our study, we now come to a time following the great flood. Noah and his wife, and his sons and their wives, are the only people to survive. Referencing Genesis 9:20-27, we see as a matter of course, Noah planted a vineyard. In time, his vineyard yielded crops and he made some wine, and apparently became drunk and lay naked inside his tent. One son, Ham, saw his father's nakedness, and, rather than preserving his father's modesty, decided to blab about it to his brothers. Shem and Japheth, respecting their father and fearing God, discreetly backed into their father's tent (so as to not see him in a compromising position) and covered their father's nakedness. Upon awakening from his drunkenness, Noah discovers what has happened. He curses Canaan, the son of Ham, condemning his entire family line to be slaves to the descendants of his brothers. He blesses Japheth and Shem, whose descendants will rule over the Canaanites.

In one curse and one joint blessing, Noah sets the course for his descendants. Genesis 10 & 11 outlines the direction of mankind and how the different clans are scattered to the ends of the earth, each clan speaking different languages from the others.

This brings us to ten generations after Noah, through the line of Shem, whose people become known as the Semites. In our text reference (Hebrews 11:8-19) we arrive at the story of Abraham.

> "By faith Abraham, when called to go to a place he would later receive as his inheritance, obeyed and went, even though he did not know where he was going. By faith he made his home in the promised land like a stranger in a foreign country; he lived in tents, as did Isaac and Jacob, who were heirs with him of the same promise.
> For he was looking forward to a city with foundations, whose architect and builder is God."

In our search for clarity it is important to thoroughly review his story as narrated to us in Genesis 12:1- 25:11, especially prior to completing the assignment at the end of Chapter 7. Abraham's life story is deep, rich, and multifaceted. It would be impossible to completely cover such voluminous information within the confines of one book, much less these three chapters. We will, however, take time to focus on various points of interest during his journey with God. These points, like rest stops on a long highway, will bring time of refreshment, new insights and new perspectives on one man's life-long, intimate relationship with the God he worships, follows and reveres.

The Call & The Promise

"The LORD had said to Abram, 'Leave your country, your people and your father's household and go to the land I will show you.
I will make you into a great nation and I will bless you;
I will make your name great, and you will be a blessing,
I will bless those who bless you, and whoever curses you I will curse;
And all peoples on earth will be blessed through you.'
So Abram left, as the LORD had told him; and Lot went with him. Abram was 75 years old when he set out from Haran. He took his wife Sarai, his nephew Lot, all the possessions they had accumulated and the people they had acquired in Haran, and they set out for the land of Canaan, and they arrived there." (Genesis 12:1-5)

Abram, a descendant of Shem, was 75 years old when was called to leave everything he knew. Reviewing the complete text of his life, we see that this is about half of his life span. He left his family identification and honorable stature to go to a land that was inhabited by the descendants of Ham, the Canaanites, who were his inferiors according to the curse of Noah. (Genesis 9:20-27)

It is important to fully recognize all that Abram leaves, in order to fully appreciate his obedience. In these times, land, crops, livestock, family connections and descendants are the measure of one's wealth and success. God is essentially asking Abram to trust that He will bless him in a way that far exceeds anything he already has, and that his name—his family name—will be well known because of God's blessings.

Further, God promises to make Abram into a great nation. Remember, Abram is 75 years old at this point, and childless. The original Hebrew, in context, states that God is literally asking Abram to walk away from the source of his life (family name and father's household), his inheritance (his rightful payment as part of the family), and the land where he is honored, and his connection to his people. God tells Abram to go to another land, the land of his cursed inferiors, the Canaanites, where he has no land of his own and where his family name carries no weight or influence. This is no small request; as a matter of fact, it's not a "request" at all. It is a calling, a command. Take a moment to understand, this is not a short stroll. This is not a "walkabout," like in the movie, *Crocodile Dundee*, where the main character knocks around on his own for a period of time of exploration. Abram is being asked to collect his considerably large holdings and move many, many miles away…by foot; there is no Mayflower Van Lines, only hoofing and "schleping" across the rugged terrain. Abram obeys and goes.

In the years that pass between the time that God first calls Abram and declares that He would make him into a great nation, and the time when He makes a covenant promise to actually give Abram the promised land, many extraordinary things take place. During a famine in the land, Abram leads his family into Egypt. Perhaps out of fear, or perhaps because he had heard of it happening in times before, Abram feels that there was a very real chance that he might be murdered so that his wife (Sarai) could become the wife on another. (I guess he didn't recall that God had said "I will bless those who bless you; and I will curse those who curse you." Genesis 12:3)

In those times, even people who didn't acknowledge the one true God still acknowledged the guidelines of culture and law. It was unlawful—and forbidden—to take a married woman as your wife, unless her husband was dead. Sarai was very beautiful, and Abram knew other men would see her allure. As a result, he and Sarai agree to lie and say she is his sister. This results in near disaster when the Pharaoh's officials see her and take her as a wife for their leader. Long story short, when Pharaoh discovers that she is Abram's wife, he confronts Abram (mild understatement), and returns Sarai to him. He also "politely" asks Abram to leave, as this little incident has caused quite an upheaval in his own home. (God inflicts all his wives and concubines so that their wombs are closed and none could have children.)

Some time after they leave, Abram and Lot decide to separate because the land will not support both of their clans. Lot chooses to settle 'near' Sodom. Eleven years later there is a war. The battles continue, and eventually Lot is taken captive by the kings who overthrow Sodom and Gomorrah. (NOTE: Lot was taken captive because he was now living *in* Sodom, not *near* Sodom.) Abram gathers men and rescues Lot. After defeating the kings who took Lot, the King of Sodom meets Abram, along with the King of Salem (Malchizedek). Abram gives Malchizedek ten percent of the spoils—the customary reward—and gives the King of Sodom everything belonging to him, except what his men required for food and payment for fighting. Abram did this so the King of Sodom would have no claim of rule over him. Abram's actions are a clear declaration that God is the only one who holds authority over him.

Confirmation of the Covenant

"After this, the word of the LORD came to Abram in a vision: 'Do not be afraid Abram. I am your shield, your very great reward.'

> But Abram said, 'O Sovereign LORD, what can you give me since I remain childless and the one who will inherit my estate is Eliezer of Damascus?'
> And Abram said, 'You have given me no children; so a servant in my household will be my heir.'
> Then the word of the LORD came to him: 'This man will not be your heir, but a son coming from your own body will be your heir.' He took him outside and said, 'Look up at the heavens and count the stars—if indeed you can count them.'
> Then he said to him, 'So shall your offspring be.' Abram believed the LORD, and he credited to him as righteousness.
> (Genesis 15:1-6)

At that time, the word of the Lord appeared to Abram in a vision, telling him his descendants would be as numerous as the stars in the heavens. Then God made a covenant promise in the vision. Abram, at God's command, cuts the carcasses of a heifer, a goat and a ram, and a dove and a pigeon into halves, placing the halves across from each other. Then he falls into a deep sleep, where God reveals "dreadful" things to him. He tells Abram that his descendants will be in a land not their own and enslaved for 400 years. Then a smoking torch passes between the pieces symbolizing a covenant between God and Abram. God promised that in the 4th generation after Abram, his descendants would take possession of the land of Canaan. As the result of yet another incomplete understanding of God's promise, Sarai decides God needs a little help with the "offspring as numerous as the stars" situation, so she gives Abram her maidservant, Hagar, to conceive a child. (Ishmael)

So— Abram has been quite busy. He is told to leave, and leaves. He lies about his wife, loses his wife, and then gets her back, along with a swift kick in the backside on his way out of town. He finds himself in the middle of wartime conflict. His nephew gets captured and must be rescued. He returns all of the King of Sodom's belongings to him, something this King

apparently couldn't accomplish on his own. He has a life-altering chat with Yahweh. He has an illegitimate child with Hagar. Can you see how God is using the events of Abram's life to change him and refine him?

Points to Ponder

There is serious transition happening here, but that's the point, isn't it? It has been my experience, both personal and through study, that life-altering, refining transition can only be accomplished through the passage of time, the challenge of upheaval, and ultimately the surrender of acceptance.

- What are some life transitions you have been called to face?
- What are some of the significant signposts in your life marking where you've been, and the things you've been required to leave behind?

We must always remember Abraham as we face our own times of "leaving." His example of obedience, even when he didn't fully understand, is inspiring and comforting. God's promises and consistent abiding love will always be the light guiding our steps as we walk…even into the unknown.

Chapter 7

A New Name

One story our girls shared in Italy that had us howling in laughter recounted how, in the Sociology class entitled, *Anatomy of the Italian Mafia*, each student had been assigned to bear the name of one of the Old World mafia families. They were to assume this new identity and meet together regularly as a family. At the end of the course, after using water guns to "off" members of rival families, one family was left standing, and my daughter was one of only three who had managed to escape, elevating herself (by mafia-style elimination) to a very high position. In any other setting we would have been embarrassingly loud with laughter; fortunately we were in Italy so we blended right in, no problem.

We truly enjoyed hearing how this infamous family name had carried weight in their little neighborhood. It really drove home to the students how a name and reputation, even a notorious one, can determine how someone is perceived.

Names are important. We spent a lot of time choosing names for each of our four children knowing it would have to last a lifetime, reflecting their place in our family. Each name chosen bears particular significance to someone special, or has a significant meaning. I remember exactly how, why and where we chose each precious name.

My place in and meaning to this family came about a bit differently. I was gifted to my family as a newborn through adoption. I remember the day my mother told me of my adoption. I was barely six years old. Still, the manner in which I was informed was so sweet and so kind, I never once questioned my identification as one who belonged to our family. As a matter of fact, it made me feel even more special as my mother recounted how much she wanted a daughter, and the lengths to which she and my father went in order to legally bind me to their home, and how she chose "Laura" as my given name. I have come to understand and reverently respect that I carry this name only because the name of someone else was willingly relinquished.

I also remember the day I married my best friend, taking on a new place and another family name. I can see the flowers and the church and my beautiful dress. As we sped away from the reception I reached into the back seat of our car and lifted a collection of cards out of a basket. Each envelope was addressed to "Mr. & Mrs. Day." For a fleeting moment I thought these cards were for my in-laws, until I remembered…that's my name now! As the years have passed, I have come to treasure this name. My parents-in-love, as I call them, are loved and respected by so many people. My father-in-law was career Navy, and as such acquired a stellar reputation as a firm but fair commander. My mother-in-law has led anything from Girl Scouts and PTA's to Naval officers' wives with all the style of a true lady. I am frequently given special courtesy because of their reputation, and I can only hope that I will continue to honor their name with my life and my endeavors.

Most importantly, I remember the day I took my place within God's family, and God changed my name. When I finally understood that my relationship with God was my responsibility and made a choice to relinquish my life in deference to God's will, I became a member of God's household. This one change

of name changed everything. I can see that now. The benefit of age and experience, combined with decades of surrender to God's transformation, has brought me to a place where I can look back and recognize the signposts.

Let us continue our time looking back at the signposts in scripture, for we will surely see that there is much importance in a name.

"I Will Change Your Name"

Continuing the story of Abram thirteen years later, God appears to Abram in another vision. God confirms the oath between them and institutes circumcision as the required symbol of this covenant. He also changes Abram's name to Abraham, Sarai's name to Sarah, and clearly states the blessing of descendants that was promised will come from Sarah, not Hagar. Abraham is now 99 years old.

Let's take time to review a few things. In the first vision (before the birth of Ishmael) a smoking firepot and blazing torch passes between the "cut" pieces of animals, which are placed directly opposite from each other. In the second vision, reference is made to those not being circumcised as being "cut off" from—or on the opposite side of—God's people and the promises made through the covenant.

The Hebrew words are:

First Vision—"batar": to cut in half, which is the word used referring to God telling Abram to cut the animals into two pieces, to separate them by putting them on opposite sides from each other.

Second Vision—"karat": to cut down, to cut off, to make covenant.

The symbolism is two-fold:

a) All males are to cut off a part of themselves as a dedication/identification (set apart) to Yahweh.

b) Whoever does not dedicate/indentify themselves to the Lord will be "cut off," finding themselves on the opposite side from God and the promises in the covenant.

While there is an intentional play on words used to clearly convey God's message to Abram, it is equally clear to Abram that God is NOT playing around. God does not play.

It has taken Abram 24 years of walking side by side with God to get to this point. Until now, God has only promised Abram these things, but there is no physical evidence that can be pointed to as actual fulfillment of the promises. God made it clear that Ishmael is not the heir He was promising. We are really beginning to see how the highs and lows of one man's life can be used to develop the virtues needed to serve God, or used to reveal the characteristics within him that need to be removed.

Now, in one of the greatest defining moments found in scripture, God blesses Abram's obedience with something that changes the course of his life forever. God changes his name.

More Than Just A Name

There are great and wondrous implications concerning God and a change of names. The weight and relevance is far, far beyond how I stated the importance of how we named our children. These names are bound within a covenant.

> *"As for me, this is my covenant with you: You will be the father of many nations. No longer will you be called Abram; your name will be Abraham, for I have made you the father of many nations. I will make you very fruitful; I will make nations of you, and kings will come from you. I will establish my covenant as an everlasting covenant between me and you and your descendants after you for the generations to come, to be your God and the God of your descendants."*
> *(Genesis 17:4-7)*

> *"...As for Sarai your wife, you are no longer to call her Sarai; her name will be Sarah. I will bless her and surely give you a son by her. I will bless her so that she will be the mother of nations; kings of peoples will come from her."*
> *(Genesis 17:15-16)*

As we can see, Yahweh makes a pivotal proclamation: their *names* will be Abraham and Sarah. The Hebrew word God uses in this case is *sem,* which means *a proper name, a designation of a person, and by extension, the fame or renown of that person.* *Sem* is a direct derivative of the name Shem and the clan of the Semites. This intentional and purposeful reference indicates to Abram a direct connection to the blessing bestowed upon his family name ten generations before. God accomplishes much more than a change of name; God, *by His intrinsic nature and sovereign authority,* grants blessing, promise, destiny, title and holy ownership within the names He intentionally bestows to the recipients.

First, He changes Abram to Abraham. God removes the title of Exalted Father (the definition of Abram) from this man who has no descendants. Next, God literally confers blessing, promise, title and holy ownership within the new name, Abraham, thereby revealing destiny within the meaning: Father of Many.

Secondly, God changes Sarai to Sarah; "princess" to "Princess," mere designation to true title, and by extension of the meaning, Mother of Royalty. The implication being she is no longer notable because of those from whom she descended; she is now notable because she will be the source through which divine royalty will arrive.

With very few exceptions, *sem* is the Hebrew word used throughout the Old Testament when referring to calling on and/or actions in the *name* of the Lord. The significance that should be meditated upon is the weight and authority carried within the act of declaring of The Lord's name. It is an awesome and humbling thing to allow this realization to ruminate within one's being.

These scriptures reveal to us those who walked before us whose actions carried the full power and authority of *El'shaddai*, God Almighty! One who would make such a declaration is definitely not playing around. Remember, God does not play.

Connecting our Past with our Future

In the New Testament, the Greek word *onoma* (also *onomazo*) is used in the same sense as the Hebrew *sem*. These intentional and purposeful references indicate to us a direct connection to the promises and blessings bestowed to every previous generation of believers, to which we also have access through Christ! The most powerful example is found in Acts 4:12:

> *"Salvation is found in no one else, for there is no other name under heaven given to men by which we must be saved."*

This is another definitive moment in history, when God's power and authority are <u>endowed to</u> and <u>embodied in</u> Jesus Christ. Jesus Christ came to earth entrusted with accomplishing reconciliation between sinful man and his Creator. As reflected within the words of this scripture, His sacrificial death, and furthermore His victory over the dominion of death by His resurrection, completely fulfills this purpose.

Further important examples of the power and authority imparted by the purposeful declaration of God's name are:

> *John 10:3- "…he calls his own sheep by name;"*
> *John 17:11- "…protect them by the power of your name;"*
> *John 20:31- "…by believing you may have life in his name;"*
> *Acts 2:38- "…baptized in the name of Jesus Christ;"*
> *1 Peter 4:16- "…praise God that you bear that name…"*
> *Ephesians 3:14 & 15- "For this reason I kneel before the Father, from whom his whole family in heaven and on earth derives its name."*

Of particular emphasis, there is also the use of the Greek word, *patria,* found in the passage quoted from Ephesians. *Patria* specifically designates, *of a family line, a clan, or a nation,* further reinforcing God's intention to identify us as His. We are, according to God's measurement, literally in His family line, part of His clan, and royal citizens of Heaven.

It's a Family Thing...

We can conclude, therefore, that when we call on the *name* of Jesus for salvation, it means we are telling God that we want to relinquish *our name.* We tell God we want a new identity, *HIS identity.* Like Abraham, God calls us to then walk away from the source of our current life, the family name of our earthly identity, including but not limited to social, ethnic and national allegiances, and embrace our heavenly citizenship. While we still possess these identities, all previous designations collectively shrink when measured against how God identifies us!

The name changing ceremony is baptism. At that time, we willingly relinquish the right to our old name. As we are baptized, we die to our old life/name and are raised into our new life/name. This is the circumcision of our hearts, which is the putting off of the sinful nature as stated in Colossians 2:11-12.

> *"*In him you were also circumcised, in the putting off of the sinful nature, not with a circumcision done by hands of men but with the circumcision done by Christ, having been buried with him in baptism and raised with him through your faith in the power of God, who raised him from the dead."*

This is our adoption into the family (*patria*) of God. Now, under the covenant promise made through Jesus' blood, *Elohim* becomes our *Abba.* (His Majesty the King becomes our Father) We wear the *name* of Jesus Christ. God has accomplished more than a simple name change. He will identify us as His own precious children, and He has made us legal heirs to the inheritance of eternal life. Through God's sovereign authority and intrinsic nature, our utmost significance is now found within the blessing, promise, title and holy ownership of wearing God's name!

New, Superior to the Old

The next time you hear the phrase, "What's in a name?" think of the words found in Revelation 2:17:

"He who has an ear, let him hear what the spirit says to the churches. To him who overcomes, I will give some hidden manna. I will also give him a white stone with a new name written on it, known only to him who receives it."

Greek references:
- leukos= white, bright gleaming
- psephos= stone, vote (cast by stones); in NT times a white stone usually meant a vote for innocence. Here it is the picture of being declared innocent.
- kainos= new, latest, in the context that the new is superior to the old
- onoma= name, title, reputation, title given
- oida= to know, recognize, understand
- lambano= to take, to be received, to be selected, to accept

Now re-written, with liberties:
"He who has an ear to hear, let him hear what the spirit says to the churches. To him who overcomes, I will give some hidden manna. I will also give a bright, gleaming, unblemished stone with a new, superior identification on it. This stone designates the owner as one whom I have judged innocent. It also identifies the owner as one who bears the name of my Royal Family. The one who possesses this stone is the only one who understands what it means to have the

honor of carrying this name. He alone is the sole owner, as I alone am his soul owner."

Chapter Post-Script

Major Life Events, High (*) and Lows (#), which God used to instill or remove character traits of Abraham:

*Obeys the Lord, leaves Ur [trust]
#Lies about Sarai, says she is his sister out of fear for is life [fear]
*Becomes wealthy in Egypt, departs taking Lot with him [blessing]
*Gives Lot the choice of the land [trust/ unselfishness]
*Rescues Lot from captivity [strength/bravery]
*Makes peace treaty with King Malchizedek of Salem [honorable]
*Covenant promised [chosen]
#Takes Hagar as a concubine to manipulate God's promise [doubt/manipulation]
#Allows Sarai to mistreat the pregnant Hagar [deference of responsibility]
(#Sarai mistreats Hagar- out of jealousy & lack of faith in God's promise)
*Covenant established with circumcision [complete obedience]
*Pleads for God to bless Ishmael too [responsibility]
#Laughs at the prospect of becoming a Father at age 99 [doubt]
#Pleads for Sodom & Gomorrah [deflection/ denial]
#Witnesses the destruction aftermath of Sodom & Gomorrah [grief]
#Becomes the Uncle of Lot's new family, through Lot's incest with his daughters [disgrace]
*Birth of Isaac [joy/ celebration]
#Influenced by Sarah to get rid of "that slave woman and her son." [hurt/embarrassment]
(# Sarah's motives were fear, jealousy, and pride)

#Sends Hagar and Ishmael away (but God gives him the "OK.") [conflicted]

*Treaty with Abimelech over land and water access in Beersheba, land of the Philistines [justice]

*Obediently offers Isaac as a sacrifice [unwavering trust and allegiance to God]

*Isaac is spared/ Ram substituted [relief/thanksgiving]

#Death of Sarah/ burial site bought from Ephron the Hittite [utter grief/ anger/ humiliation]

On a personal note:

I am both encouraged and humbled by the study of Abraham. It has been taught to me for many years, three decades actually. Prior to the project before you, I had not really taken a deeper look at this man's frailties; I had not placed my heart within the boundaries of his hopes and disappointments, his inner longings or his struggle to grasp a solid understanding of his God's master plan.

It is only through this study that I have come to deeply identify with Abraham and Sarah. No, I would never be arrogant enough to think my life story could possibly have such far-reaching implications for mankind. The connection, at least for me, is in the imperfections, and Abraham had many. Oddly, perhaps, I find that comforting. I indeed find it comforting to know that the God of all Creation holds true to His promises in spite of one's lack of understanding, even in spite of faithless actions based on doubt.

None of who I am today would be possible without the cumulative effect of all my life's failures and victories. The "me" I am now is vastly different from the "me" in the time of my first calling at nineteen, and markedly different from the "me" of even a year ago. God has woven an infinite, majestic tapestry out of the threads that bind our life-journey together, and I am just now beginning to take hold of a tiny edge. I see through the life of Abraham that even in my deepest moments of fear and doubt, and

I have had many, God never abandons me. In fact it is the exact opposite. God moves even closer to me. He doesn't remove the natural consequences of poor decisions in my life. Conversely, He loves me more intimately. By my willing surrender, God expands within me, taking permanent residence in rooms of my spirit that I had previously closed off from Him, denying Him access to those parts of me that needed to be left behind. Then, like a loud thunder victoriously heralding the introduction to each deeper phase in our relationship, Abba boldly continues to reveal His love to me, and I find myself loving God more than I ever thought possible.

As I write this I am left wondering... how did I miss it? Until now, how could I have possibly missed this amazing epiphany? Fortunately for me there is this story, this balm for my soul, this Abraham. This one man through whom God blessed all nations is also a man who lied, manipulated, doubted, deflected, deferred and flat out dropped the ball. He also was a man who committed, obeyed, rescued, provided, deeply loved and persevered. God loved all of who Abraham was. And God loves all of who I am as well.

There it is. God loves me. God has made a covenant promise to me through the blood of Jesus Christ, and He remains true to His promise as we walk together. I'm not expected to be perfect; God is *perfecting* me. I won't always get it right, but because I trust in God, it will *be made right through His power!*

That's a whole new level of faith for this weary traveler. I am just so deeply grateful for the journey. And in the end, may I be found to have, "... breathed her last and died at a good, old age, an old woman full of years; and she was gathered to her people. Her children buried her. And after her death, God blessed her children, who then lived on in faith." [Broad liberties adapted from Genesis 25:7-11]

Points to Ponder

YOUR NAME AND YOUR CALLING—TIME TO DRAW SOME PARALELLS:

- The calling of Abraham = What calling of ours? (Romans 8:28-39)
- Abraham left behind what? = What are we leaving behind? (Romans 6:4-14; Colossians 3:1-17; Philippians 3:7-14)
- What is the benefit of obedience for Abraham? = What is the benefit of ours? (Matthew 19:28-30)
- How is Abraham an Alien? = How are we Aliens? (1Peter 2:9-12; Philippians 3:20)
- Compare the <u>intended</u> similarities between physical circumcision and our spiritual circumcision. (Colossians 2:9-15)
- As God changed Abram's name to call him Abraham, what will we be called? (1 John 3:1)

Chapter 8
The Waiting

I adore small children. Their unaffected nature is so refreshing. Their unbridled exuberance is a joy. When my husband and I were ushered into the grandparents club, we had no idea that our initial mountaintop experience could possibly be topped. Every day, however, and every experience with our "grands" only solidifies our understanding that God is truly amazing, and we can hardly wait for the next grand to arrive.

One thing is consistent among our little ones. They have absolutely no concept of time. Their lack of understanding is just too cute. Our first grand, Brooklyn, keeps us laughing constantly. She will say that she will see us in five tomorrows, or that she remembers something that happened last year as "last Monday ago." While we are convinced she is a baby genius—all of our grands are geniuses—this one little hiccup in the system makes her even more adorable. As a natural result, though, there are some challenges when any kind of waiting is required.

I would love to proclaim that this phenomenon resolves upon reaching adulthood. As I have firmly committed to a truthful lifestyle, I simply cannot do this. The impatience of those who surround me in various situations serves as daily confirmation of this fact. You all know whom I'm talking about. As a matter of fact, I may be talking about you: The Heavy Sigher, who is so obviously disgruntled that anyone dare to precede her in the grocery checkout line; The Tailpipe Rider, who is convinced that he personally owns every road, and especially the exact piece of asphalt directly under *your* tires, which he is determined to reclaim even if you die in the process; The Teen Eye Roller, who knows more than anyone on earth, but especially more than the person who at this very moment has the unmitigated gall to try to correct a rude behavior, or heaven forbid, actually point out that her way too revealing t-shirt looks like it came from Baby Gap; The No Filters Talker, who knows just barely enough about the U.S. Constitution to avail himself of his right to "colorful" free speech, and is ever so happy to use it to get his way—right now.

It's not completely their fault either. We live in a world of drive-thru gratification, electronic mail, and instant messaging. There is more than anecdotal evidence that this current generation no longer uses wristwatches because the time is posted on their cell phones but struggle more than any previous generation with grasping the concept of being on time. In other words, they refuse to wait for what is theirs now, but have no problem making you wait for what is yours. And there is effort in keeping my own patience in check. Of course I'd rather get the nice dinner at a restaurant now than spend the time and energy to produce it myself, duh!

So how do we achieve balance? How can we learn to appreciate, even welcome, the lessons that come with waiting? Friends, I can confidently tell you I don't have all the answers. The words in this book were never meant to be the "end all" and "be all" in the principles for a Christian lifestyle. I can, however, tell you what I have observed in others who, by trusting in God and waiting on His answers, have arrived at a depth of faith and peace they never knew existed. I can also tell you the process by which I surrendered impatience and now embrace what I call *The Waiting*.

God, In a Box

The enthusiasm experienced within the first few years following my commitment to Christ was wide-eyed to say the least. I was sure I had a grasp on the how-to's and was self-assured in my boundary lines. Yes, God was nicely confined to my imaginary little box, and I was completely comfortable this way. My faith hit some challenges, though, over a several-years period of church splits, protracted arguments over doctrine vs. tradition, and witnessing people of seemingly good character behave not only hurtfully but also maliciously. Before this time, I had been a spiritual eye-roller of sorts. I had strong admiration for other Christians who seemed unswerving in their biblical knowledge and spiritual conviction. When any long-time Christian proposed that perhaps one thing or another was not completely cut and dried… I rolled my eyes. It was like, "… Oh brother, here we go again with the wishy-washy willie-nillie…" The truth is, the unknown made me uncomfortable. No matter how wise any of these kind folks were, my heart wasn't ready to receive the wisdom within their words.

Looking back now, I get it. Real life itself takes you down the road to wisdom, and these people had experienced a lot of real life. Other than that, there is no "instant" involved, no quick fix. God was never in my box, or any box for that matter. It takes the cumulative effect of many things to shake one out of the trance of boxed-up-assurance and move one into the wide-open spaces of this singular understanding: The only real assurance found in life is found in trusting God.

There is one thing I can put my finger on, though. The one thing that has really drawn me close to God is this: the hospital waiting room. We've sat in waiting rooms because of tragic teen car accidents. We've sat because of untimely heart attacks. We've sat for young and old alike. There have been births and deaths, and everything in between, and the one common factor is *The Waiting*. Of course, waiting with others for their answers hasn't affected me nearly as deeply as waiting for my own. And the one that cut the cord to self assurance completely was when we were a day away, maybe even just hours away, from losing our daughter, Anna.

The Call, and My Calling

Ironically, my calling to trust God more fully began with a phone call. That call came at 3:30am on a Friday. The words shook me out of sleep to completely awake: "We believe your daughter has aseptic meningitis." Our twins were in their sophomore year of college in Nashville and a weekend away from first semester finals. Our Anna, a Division-I cross country runner, fell ill while on a sorority-sponsored trek to a local comedy club. Her Resident Advisor and two sorority sisters rushed her to the emergency room with a dangerously high fever, headache and stiff neck. The doctor who called me excused himself and hung up before I was able to fully process all the information: She's been here since 12:30a.m.; She's getting a spinal tap; Don't go anywhere yet; I'll call back when I know. At 5a.m. I was already packing a suitcase when the phone rang. The only thing I remember next was being in my car. I made the 12-hour drive to Nashville in ten hours.

That was the beginning of *The Waiting*. I waited for updates in my car. My husband waited for updates at home and would fly up if he were needed. We based that decision on the information we were given: She's holding her own. She's stable. We have it under control. Yes, it is serious. No, it is not life threatening at this time.

May I say a word or two about the gift of having a child attend a small Christian university? One of my daughter's teachers sped to the hospital and became surrogate parent until I arrived. She was able to be liaison between the medical staff and me and could reassure me in my anxiety. She was the only one who had a gut feeling that things were worse than what I was being told. She

knew my daughter well and could see that both her color and her disposition were fading.

When I arrived and literally ran to the floor where I was directed, I almost fainted when I saw the name of the wing where Anna was taken: Oncology. Fighting panic, I pushed through to her room to find my frail little girl heavily sedated and as white as the sheets. Sensing my fear, the nurse on duty quickly explained to me that the cancer treatment wing was the most sterile in the building, and therefore the best place for Anna. That calmed my nerves, at least temporarily.

Her sister, Ashley, was a near permanent fixture by her side, leaving only to take a shower. I was still being assured that she was going to be all right, and for the next day and a half that seemed to be true. My husband would find a flight when we were sure of when she'd be released, and he would help drive all three of us home.

Early Sunday morning, however, everything hit the fan. For no apparent reason the headaches returned with a vengeance, and the pain medications held little control. Anna had no reserves available to hold herself upright, and a new battery of tests began. I phoned my husband to no avail, and then reached an elder at our church, our dear friend Tom, as services were beginning. My husband, an elder as well, was addressing the congregation with announcements and thanking everyone for their prayers. As he stepped down, Tom escorted him as calmly as possible from the building directly to his car, filling him in on the way. Thanks to cell phones, by the time he reached home and packed a small bag, his flight was confirmed and he narrowly had time to make his plane. He arrived to Anna's room almost as white as she was, but his presence alone brought the first smile from our daughter I had seen, and she rallied for a bit.

After a conference with the doctor, again we began *The Waiting*. The President of the university stopped in. While he prayed with my husband, his wife walked over to the bed, held Anna's hand and stroked her hair and prayed like no one I've ever seen before. This was a woman with precious children of her own, a strong woman of God, who refused to let illness overtake us. I will never forget that moment.

I Give You My Daughter

The ebb and flow of serious illness, its impact on the patient and the effect on those who love her, cannot be accurately calculated. The full understanding of it only comes through the process. Again, we had two days of progress. Ashley came and went according to her scheduled finals and was allowed to keep her phone on her desk, just in case. Anna enjoyed brief visits from friends, then slept for hours from the taxation on her body. She ate a few things, then would struggle with nausea. She would walk the 50 feet to the large waiting room where her Dad was taking calls, trailing her I.V.'s, then barely be able to walk 5 feet to the bathroom. The tests revealed nothing of substance, and so they continued. So did the headaches. Then everything came to a halt. She was completely unable to function. Anna's doctor told us he didn't know what else to do. There were only two more things to try, and that would determine everything.

Without getting too technical, the doctors hit her system with what we prayed would be a knock out punch of drugs. At the same time, they made the conclusion that she also had a leak of spinal fluid from multiple tests, and the doctors would attempt a blood patch to stop the leaks. We were told one of us could accompany her to the procedure, but when the time came we were told we absolutely could not. In one moment of fear and frustration, I can still remember my husband saying, "We have to give them our daughter." We were asked to lay our child down, surrendering her to the doctor, the one who held her life in his hands, and wait.

That was the day. That was the one single hour of my life when God moved so close to me, so completely to my aid and comfort that I will never be the same. In the hour that we waited, I completely understood that while God can do anything, the veil

between heaven and earth is a mere step away, and sometimes people must leave us. I knew because I have personally sat as a spectator in this situation before, but never as a key player. My husband, Ashley and I sat on the razor thin edge of an abyss, looking straight down into bottomless despair knowing that at any moment we could be sent plummeting. There was no praying, only the complete stillness of God's presence moving within our very souls acknowledging our profound need. I had heard people talk before of being "in the throne room," and definitely believed I had experienced it most of my life, until then. Perhaps my heart had been in the throne room before, but this was the first time I truly felt my body physically enter that room. I can't explain how, but for that single, solitary hour of my life I knew I was at the feet of the God I worship. I lost myself in trust, and waited for His scepter to grant the only thing that mattered: Anna's life.

This is the waiting that matters. It is this kind of trust that enables us to wait at God's feet and watch Him just be God. This is the waiting that washes us in grace and peace, binds our hearts with that of our Creator, and leaves His wisdom within us. I can't believe I ever rolled my eyes at this.

When the door jolted open and the only one standing there was the doctor, my husband grabbed my hand and my heart sank. Less than a second later, a beaming Anna was wheeled into the room, and we literally shouted for joy! The procedure was a complete success, and the headaches were gone. Within the next 24 hours the drugs threw the knock out punch we had prayed for, and by the following weekend we were driving home.

None of us will ever be the same. We have seen God move powerfully, and we have experienced His power in the most intimate of ways. I do not wish to overstep, or in any way imply that this life event will have such far-reaching implications as that of Abraham's call to sacrifice Isaac. The parallel for me, though, is found in the discovery of trust. Let us examine God's word and see if we can draw comparisons.

Give Me Your Only Son

"Some time later God tested Abraham. He said to him, 'Abraham!' 'Here I am,' he replied. Then God said, 'Take your son, your only son, Isaac, whom you love, and go to the region of Moriah. Sacrifice him there as a burnt offering on one of the mountains I will tell you about.'

Early the next morning Abraham got up and saddled his donkey. He took with him two of his servants and his son Isaac. When he had cut enough wood for the burnt offering, he set out for the place God had told him about. On the third day Abraham looked up and saw the place in the distance. He said to his servants, 'Stay here with the donkey while I and the boy go over there. We will worship and then we will come back to you.'

Abraham took the wood for the burnt offering and placed it on his son Isaac, and he himself carried the fire and the knife. As the two of them went on together, Isaac spoke up and said to his father, 'Father?'

'Yes my son,' Abraham replied.

'The fire and wood are here,' Isaac said, 'but where is the lamb for the burnt offering?'

Abraham answered, 'God himself will provide the lamb for the burnt offering, my son.' And the two of them went on together.

When they reached the place God had told him about, Abraham built an altar there and arranged the wood on it. He bound his son Isaac and laid him on the altar, on top of the wood. Then he reached out his hand and took the knife to slay his son. But the angel of the LORD called out to him from heaven, 'Abraham! Abraham!'

'Here I am,' he replied.

'Do not lay a hand on the boy,' he said. 'Do not do anything to him. Now I know that you fear God, because you have not withheld from me your son, your only son.'

Abraham looked up and there in the thicket he saw a ram caught by its horns. He went over and took the ram

and sacrificed it as a burnt offering instead of his son. So Abraham called that place The LORD Will Provide. And to this day it is said, 'On the mountain of the LORD it will be provided."
(Genesis 22:1-14)

After the time we've spent walking side by side with Abraham, it seems like our whole posture is changing, and for the better. Abraham's life story reveals many different facets of God's being. Sitting at God's table and feasting on the fine, multi-course spiritual nourishment provided by Abraham's example gives us a real sense of how God was changing and building this man's character through the many challenges he faced. Ultimately, as he was wholeheartedly willing to sacrifice his only son, Isaac, the son through whom the fulfillment of God's covenant promise was to come, Abraham finally grasps the very nature and purpose of God in regard to himself!

This, without question, is the event that solidified Abraham's understanding of who God is and how God's sovereignty prevails. First, we must clearly understand that God, who knows all things, foreknew each time Abraham would either succeed or fail, and thus revealed the human weaknesses within His servant <u>to His servant.</u> I understand this is a radical concept, but don't fret just yet. Try to allow this new point of view to ruminate within you a bit.

Let's remember, God is not frivolous. Certainly God is lavish, but nothing He does is without absolute purpose. The test to sacrifice Isaac wasn't to prove Abraham's love to God. The Sovereign Ruler of the universe knows all things, including men's hearts, and we must accept that God knew Abraham's heart completely. As Abraham sat on the razor-thin edge of the abyss, his hand held high in preparation to sacrifice his son, God held his hand back. That exact moment revealed to Abraham how much as a servant of God he had changed and grown. It is precisely when God returns Isaac back to him that Abraham experiences for the first time how deeply and intimately God loves him, and would always honor His promises.

Ultimately, the test to sacrifice Isaac achieved exactly what God's will ordained. The length of time Abraham spent waiting for fulfillment of God's promise was incredibly long. Somewhere within the make-up of Abraham must have remained the possibility that he would focus on the evidence of fulfillment: the gift of Isaac. God was accomplishing a permanent shift of vision by forcing Abraham to focus not on the gift, but The Giver. This is precisely what God desires to accomplish within us through *The Waiting*. God asks us to shift our focus from the gift we desire so deeply to a deeper trust and dependence on The Giver of all good things. When we ask to receive that which is created—a child, a spouse, a house, a job, a cure—our only focus should be on The Creator of all things.

We are left, now, wondering how we can reflect on this and how we can apply the lesson to our own walk with God. How can we arrive at a place where trust is all that is asked of us, and we willingly obey? Again, I submit that I don't have all the answers. The life of Abraham reveals that he is not perfect, and he does have times of doubt. His arrival at this destination should not be our focus. We must expand our vision to receive the entire journey. Looking back, Abraham's walk with God reveals a divine pattern of providence. God provided Abraham everything he needed, exactly when he needed it, even allowing him to experience suffering and deep emotional pain. (Losing Sarai to Pharaoh's household, banishing Hagar and Ishmael, rescuing Lot, and living with the shame of Lot's incest to name a few.) This must be accepted before we will ever get a clear vision of where God is leading us. Abraham did not arrive overnight at the foot of God's throne with a trusting heart willing to sacrifice to such an extent. The lessons learned along the way came at a very high price. The Abraham who was willing to sacrifice his only son was only forged in the refining fires of trusting and waiting.

Points to Ponder

- Like Sarah, how have you tried to "fix things" on your own, with bad results?
- How much power do you possess to "fix," compared to God's power?
- List some of the major events in your life that have changed you and your willingness to trust God more fully. Can you see the pattern of providence by God?
- What are the "Isaacs" in your life, the things most precious to you?
- If you were asked to lay them down and wait for God to provide, could you?
- What specifically stands in the way to your complete trust in God?

Chapter 9
The Other Side of Danger

Busy Sarah, Lazy Susan

I truly believe that the reason I love family gatherings is because of the family traditions that have resulted from them. One such tradition treasured by all of our children is our annual beach trek on the Fourth of July. With barely an exception, we have joined my in-laws at their home in Florida's panhandle every summer since my husband and I married over thirty years ago. The sugar-white beaches, coastal-dune lakes and emerald-green Gulf of Mexico have become as natural a part of our being as our fingerprints and blood types.

My husband's parents, Earl and Sarah, frequented these beaches as children and teens starting in the late 1930's. During Earl's tenure in the Navy, he would take every available vacation day but a few, request them in a summer-time lump sum, and drive his brood here in the family station wagon every year of their lives. (All but the years when stationed overseas, obviously.) The tradition has been passed to his children, who each made the pilgrimage for a week during summer breaks with their own families, the only exception being the one who actually moved to live here permanently. Now, seventy-five years after Earl and Sarah's first visits, our small grandchildren, their great-grandchildren, are enjoying this experience, too. I marvel at how the allure of this beach is so dependable and even predictable across age, gender, and generation.

This tradition is woven together with many threads, each lending color, texture and pattern. One thread in particular comes at the end of every day, when Sarah serves dinner. Every meal is anxiously anticipated, the aromas wafting from the kitchen for several hours beforehand, as Sarah busies herself as well as two ovens, and usually all four stovetop burners. The whirl of activity teases the hunger within every sun-weary beach bum in the house. Then, to our delight, every dish is placed in the center of the grand round table, on the Lazy Susan, signaling dinnertime has arrived.

When dinner is finished and the last of the biscuits has been claimed, we all partake in what truly satisfies the hunger of our souls: the family stories. As the family has grown and the generations expanded, extra tables have been added to our floor plan. But as the stories begin, every chair arrives at the round table; every loved one is accommodated, as this is a time no one wants to miss.

Tell Me the Story

Each person has their favorite and though we all know the stories well, we always long to hear them again in this setting. Generally speaking, we begin with the funny ones: My husband's annoying his older sister resulting in pizza dough in his face and hair; A sister's "colorful" outburst upon getting her hands caught in a double-hung window; The baby sister's self-inflicted pixie haircut, from waist-length hair, after finding her mother's sewing shears; The middle sister's church pew knock-out punch to my husband when she mistook a teasing purse tug from her Dad as coming from her brother; Arriving home in Charleston

to find hundreds of frogs launching themselves everywhere after a neighbor-boy had been slipping them through the mail slot for their entire month of vacation; The walloping of the same neighbor-boy by the eldest sister as a result of said frog prank; The tiny tiger-striped kitten the baby sister just had to have, sweetly naming him "Buffy", which eventually grew into a deranged, feline-serial-killing-menace that nearly snuffed out my husband and his mother as they transported it to the vet's office to…well… send it to kitty heaven; How all four now-grown children fight fainting at the smell of rubbing alcohol, the result of two years in the Philippines and the endless injections required to update their immune systems (oddly enough, one sister became a nurse…go figure); the falling off the dock; the candy stash in the planter; "Shadow," the surfboard riding black Labrador; "Sam," the beach bum dog that refused to be left behind if anyone was skiing on the lake. These and more are the stories loved and treasured by all.

The Storm, Before and After

As the stories continue, we shift to the more serious: the earthquakes in the Philippines; the hasty exit at the shifting of power in Guantanamo Bay, Cuba; the loss of dear Uncle Harold. There are so many stories that make up our family tapestry. The one that is told with a hush in the room is of the time when my father-in-law rode out a hurricane at sea, on a disabled floating dry dock being towed by another ship. One can still see the stress in his face as he recounts the radio banter between them. The force of the winds and the size of the waves threatened to sink the dry dock many times, and he repeatedly asked for the towline to be extended. Each time he requested, the commander of the other ship reassured them they already had enough line, and that they would be fine.

Only after the crisis had passed could they reveal the whole story. The towline had broken on the tow-ship's end, and there had been a frenzy of activity in the throes of the storm to re-attach it before they lost the dry dock. The commander knew that this information would cause fear and panic on the other vessel. There was no benefit to their knowing, and there was too much to lose should fear overtake them. Every man's life was in his hands. His only choice was to save them the only way available—reattaching the reduced length of tow line—and he was fully committed to reassuring them until the storm had passed. The amount of line they had would have to be exactly enough. Every time the call came saying they needed more, he calmly replied, "You have to trust me. We've got you and we're not letting you go. It's going to be fine. I've given you all you need."

Have you ever faced storms that threaten to overtake you? Have there ever been circumstances of such magnitude that you find yourself enslaved by fear? Has there ever been an event so overpowering that panic took you in its grip, and you couldn't see a way out? Have you ever asked, "Why me?" Nearly everyone I've ever asked answers, "Yes." Nearly everyone I've asked was fearful when they saw their storm coming. Everyone I've asked, however, has a strong understanding of what was accomplished through the crisis…from the perspective of "after." Storms, unfortunately, are a natural part of life. If you haven't already faced this kind of crisis then brace yourself, because real life can turn dangerously scary in a hurry, and sometimes there is only one way out.

The Road to Slavery

> *"By faith Isaac blessed Jacob and Esau in regard to their future.*
> *By faith Jacob, when he was dying, blessed each of Joseph's sons, and worshipped as he leaned on the top of his staff.*
> *By faith Joseph, when his end was near, spoke about the exodus of the Israelites from Egypt and gave special instructions about his bones.*
> *By faith Moses' parents hid him for three months after he was born, because they saw he was no ordinary child, and they were not afraid of the king's edict.*

By faith Moses, when he had grown up, refused to be known as the son of Pharaoh's daughter. He chose to be mistreated along with the children of God rather than to enjoy the pleasures of sin for a short time. He regarded disgrace for the sake of Christ as of greater value than the treasures of Egypt, because he was looking ahead to his reward. By faith he left Egypt, not fearing the king's anger; he persevered because he saw him who is invisible. By faith he kept the Passover and the sprinkling of blood, so that the destroyer of the firstborn would not touch the firstborn of Israel." (Hebrews 11:20-28)

"As the sun was setting, Abram fell into a deep sleep, and a thick and dreadful darkness came over him. The LORD said to him, "Know for certain that your descendants will be strangers in a country not their own, and they will be enslaved four hundred years. But I will punish the nation they serve as slaves, and afterward they will come out with great possessions." (Genesis 15:12-14)

In this chapter and the next, we will examine God's deliverance of the Israelites from two different perspectives. First, we will review the life of Moses and the journey of his relationship with Yahweh. Second, we will take a deeper look at the Israelite people, searching for new insights and fresh inspiration from the perspective of how they faced slavery and their ultimate liberation.

It has been four generations (four hundred years) since God fulfilled the promises of the covenant with Abraham, through the birth of Isaac. Following Isaac were Jacob (renamed "Israel" by God), and Joseph, born to Jacob in his old age. After being sold into slavery by his jealous brothers and thrown into jail by the lies of a deceitful woman, Joseph eventually is placed in a high position in Egypt, second only to Pharaoh. This is accomplished through the power of God working in Joseph, manifested in dream interpretation.

Next, as the result of a severe famine, Joseph saves his entire family, including the brothers who betrayed him, and they all move to Egypt where Joseph arranges for their provision and protection. Joseph does this because he clearly understands that through all the adversity he faced, God ultimately intended him to be in that very place for that very purpose.

As the famine continues for many years, the children of Israel living in Egypt under Pharaoh's rule have no choice but to sell themselves into servitude in order to buy food for their families. (Gen. 15:12-14, Ex. 47:13-27) This brings us to a time approximately 200 years after the death of Joseph when there is a new Pharaoh who knows nothing about Joseph and that he is a special servant of God possessing a special blessing. It is also a time when the bitterness of the Egyptians towards the Israelite people reaches unbearable intensity, as they resent having to share the land and what little food there is, and the Israelites are forced into bone-breaking labor.

The scripture references then illustrate what happens when Moses enters the picture and follows a path that leads him face to face with Yahweh. To begin, Moses is born and then hidden in a basket coated with pitch along the banks of the Nile River. He is found by Pharaoh's daughter and adopted as her own. He grows up in Pharaoh's household and takes his place among the elite. While out one day, he kills an Egyptian for the abuse being inflicted on a Hebrew slave. In fear of retribution from Pharaoh, he flees to Midian. At this time he is approximately forty years old. There, he is accepted into the family of Reuel (Jethro), marries Zipporah and has a son, Gershom. Moses lives in Midian with his wife and her family for another forty years. During this time, the king of Egypt dies, and the children of Israel cry out to God because of the harsh slavery to which they are subjected. God is deeply concerned about His children and remembers the covenant He made with Abraham, the promise to punish the nation his descendents serve as slaves, and the promise to free them. (*Referencing Genesis 15:14, Exodus 2:1-25, and Acts 7:23-29*)

You Can't Hide From God

This brings us to a time when Moses is tending the flocks, and comes upon what the Bible calls a "strange sight": a burning bush that doesn't get consumed by the fire. From this bush, God calls out to Moses and tells him to remove his sandals, for the place where he is standing is holy ground. Moses falls face down, not wanting to look upon God's face. While his reactions seem normal at first glance, let's dig deeper. Remember that the event that caused Moses to leave Egypt in the first place was the act of murder. He may have had fear of Pharaoh, but the burning bush brings fear to a whole new level: he is facing God! Moses also has an immediate understanding of the definition of holy ground. It isn't holy because of where it is, it is holy because of who is there: Yahweh.

God tells Moses that He has heard the cry of the Israelites, and He wants Moses to go free them. He also states that Pharaoh will not release them unless compelled by God's mighty hand, but that God will make it happen. The only thing Moses hears, though, is that he is the one who is being sent into the turmoil.

So now we have a conversation between Moses and God that spans Exodus 4:1-17, where Moses clearly sees the storm clouds of life gathering on the horizon. Fear causes him to try to avoid being a responsible follower of God, dodging that which he is being commanded to do. He does what we all do when we don't want to obey God's word. He tries to weasel out of it.

First he brings up his lack of CREDIBILITY. He challenges a direct command from Yahweh because of the flaws he knows about himself—how he lived as an Egyptian and is known as a murderer. God answers by telling him, according to the Hebrew words and the context of the original translation, to tell the Israelites that "Existence" sent him. He is literally telling Moses to state that the source of all existence is his credibility. Problem #1 solved.

Next, Moses tries to hide behind his INABILITY. He whines that he has no skills, that he has no game...that he's not a *"play-ah."* The English translation states that he says he is not eloquent but is slow of speech and tongue. When I researched the original language of this passage, I laughed so hard that at one point, no sound was coming from me! What Moses really said was that no matter what he means to say, the opposite comes out. He also says that his difficulty speaking is so severe that sometimes what comes out of his mouth sounds like the noise of a wild animal. Really. I'm not kidding. Friends, this man has some real issues, and I'm not talking about his speech. The extent to which he is willing to disobey God brings about some slow simmering anger from Yahweh. God is losing patience, and fast.

The scriptures say Yahweh answers Moses with this: "Who gave man his mouth? Who makes him deaf or mute? Who gives him sight or makes him blind? Is it not I, the LORD? Now go; I will help you speak and tell you what to say." God just rebuked Moses, and it was harsh! He basically said, "I am God and you are not, and don't you get impudent with me, mister." Problem #2 solved.

As a last ditch effort, Moses tries using IMMOBILITY: I can't go. Moses digs his heels in and tells God to please send someone else. This is when God burns with anger and basically tells Moses, "I'm sending your brother Aaron to help you, but you are going. And NOW." Problem #3 solved, end of discussion.

Moses accepts his calling and consecrates himself by circumcision, accepting the physical designation of God's ownership, and the spiritual designation of one called in service to Yahweh. Then he goes.

Gale Force Warnings

As the storm of confrontation gains strength, Moses obeys God and goes to Pharaoh. He asks Pharaoh to let the Israelites go, but to no avail. God already made it clear this would happen.

God—Yahweh—now makes an astonishing declaration, which serves as a warning to both Pharaoh and the Israelites.

> "...Now you will see what I will do to Pharaoh: because of my mighty hand he will let them go; because of my mighty hand he will drive them out of his country...
> I am the LORD. I appeared to Abraham, to Isaac and to Jacob as God Almighty, but by my name the LORD I did not make myself known to them. I also established my covenant with them to give them the land of Canaan, where they lived as aliens. Moreover, I have heard the groanings of the Israelites, whom the Egyptians are enslaving, and I have remembered my covenant...
> Therefore say to the Israelites: 'I am the LORD, and I will bring you out from under the yoke of the Egyptians. I will free you...
> ...I will redeem you with outstretched arm...I will take you as my own people...I will be your God...I am the LORD your God...I will bring you to the land I swore with uplifted hand to give to Abraham...I will give it to you...I AM THE LORD." (Exodus 6: 1- 8, abbreviated)

God has shown himself to Moses and has patiently waited for Moses to accept his calling. He has defined who He is, demonstrated who He is, and proclaimed His divine purpose. Moses has argued, hedged and avoided what God is asking him to do. In a final resolution, God basically says, "Oh yes you will go!"

When all God has said comes to pass, and Pharaoh refuses to release God's people, Moses is again filled with doubt and despair. He is basically wanting more than God has already given him. Here is where God makes his authority and intent perfectly clear: You have to trust me. I've got you, and I'm not letting you go. It's going to be fine. I've given you all you need.

The English translation of the original text, I feel, loses some of the strength and foreboding when God speaks. After examination, I have taken the liberty of rephrasing the passage to try to emphasize all God was implying as He made this declaration:

> "I am Yahweh, God of power and might. I am your deliverer and I will avenge the wrongs committed against you. I will take possession of you, so that you will be by my side. You are my countrymen. I will now show Pharaoh exactly how wrong he is to possess something that is MINE, and he will pay dearly."

The Search for Perspective

The battle lines are drawn, my friends. God is going to move, and it's going to be an enormous storm when He exerts Himself to accomplish His will. (Exodus chapters 6 through 15:18) I suggest that you take some time to review the entirety of the text we have been (and will be) referencing, so that you can have a clear understanding of how God is moving through this storm. It is important to really meditate on how God increases the intensity of the crisis. Without reviewing the whole story, you can never fully envision what *"stretching out my mighty arm"* really means or appreciate the point at which God shields His people from the consequences of the plagues.

Points to Ponder

Reviewing the text also affords us an opportunity to pay special attention to ways in which we can apply the lessons to our own walk with God. The open and honest examination of our own hearts and habits, though, will not be easy. Prayerfully and reverently search for the parallels between Moses' life and your walk with God in the following:

- When facing a direct call to obedience from God, how have you allowed your CREDIBILITY and INABILITY to stand in the way of obeying?
- Where have you hidden behind IMMOBILITY, and outright refused to move from actions or habits that are in direct disobedience to God?
- In Exodus, where does God exert His power? Where has God exerted power on your behalf?
- In Exodus, where does God provide all that is needed? Where has He provided for you?
- As the situation progresses and unfolds, where does Moses become stronger and bolder? When do his actions reflect that he has full trust and confidence in God? How does that apply to the storms of your life? Do your actions reflect a full trust and confidence in God?
- Compare how Moses has changed
  1. from the man he was when the storm clouds were approaching—God's calling him to service.
  2. through the storms—obeying God in the face of complete opposition.
  3. after the storm—as displayed in Moses' song of praise to Yahweh, his deliverer.
- How have your storms changed you and your depth of trust in God?
- Can you see, through the perspective of looking back, the power of God working in your life; the providence of God, even in the storms; the purpose of God in refining you to become the servant He is calling you to be?

Chapter 10

The Impossible & The Impossible

The Rest of the Story

The story of towing the floating dry dock is remarkable in many ways, none so much as from the perspective of the men who were actually on the dock during that horrendous storm. It is obvious from the radio conversation that my father-in-law was fighting fear and panic. You have to believe that every time he was told not to worry, he was thinking, "That's easy for you to say. You're not the one with no engine and no power to do anything. You're not the one at the mercy of the one who's leading you in life-threatening circumstances!"

According to accounts following the storm, the rest of the men on the vessel were definitely feeling the same way. They were not privy to the verbal exchange that took place and the reassurances that they were going to be safe. They had no way of knowing that the ship towing them had complete control. From their perspective—the giant waves threatening to swamp the ship and the increasing force of the winds—they were doomed. I'm fairly certain that faced with the same situation and the same limited information, I'd feel doomed, too.

The Perspective of the Persecuted

In Chapter 9, we walked a long journey with Moses as God called him to deliver the Israelite people from the bondage of Egypt. The many examples of how God uses difficult situations to develop strength and character in His chosen servants are both significant and inspiring. The God of Abraham, Isaac and Jacob is the same God whose only begotten son purchased our lives through the shedding of his blood. Elohim, El'shaddai, Yahweh- this is the same God who desires an intimate relationship with each of us as we journey through this life. The demonstration of God's patience with Moses is particularly significant to us, as we all tend to avoid embracing the full measure of our divine calling: the role of ambassadors or emissaries bearing God's message to a lost world.

Next, it is also important to understand this: God is unwavering as He moves towards accomplishing His purpose. It becomes clear that God can accomplish His purpose with or without us, but His desire is to include us in the process. It is within this process, therefore, that God intends to change the very essence of who we are, and accompany us to the place where we are transformed, strengthened and refined. Intimacy with God and service to God are where we are going; testing and transformation is the road by which we travel.

As we continue our study, we now change our focus to the Israelites. Let us enter our time of examination gently and reverently. We do not want to make the mistake of assuming the position of judges or critics. In Exodus 6:9, the Bible states that the Israelites didn't believe what Moses was telling them about their deliverance from bondage because of their discouragement and the cruelty with which they were being treated. Remember, during the time when Moses was born, there was even an edict to kill all male Hebrew babies. Therefore let us render compassion to them as we walk through their experience together. Bear in mind that these people have been in a foreign land working as slaves,

brutally exploited, with no one as their advocate — and it has been this way for nearly 400 years. It has been a long time since anyone has seen God make Himself known; these folks don't even know anyone *who knows anyone* who has seen God. Their situation is about to change, however, and their world is about to be turned upside down.

Inside the Storm

God has commanded Moses, now about 80 years old, to tell Pharaoh to let the people go. But God also says that Pharaoh's heart will be hardened by God, and he will not let them go. God has also stated that Pharaoh will pay for this. It is important to understand what is meant in the concept of God hardening Pharaoh's heart. This is not saying that God is controlling Pharaoh's mind, making him refuse. The translation of the original text uses phrasing and words that mean it will be like wringing out the liquid that is in a cloth or a rag. God will literally apply harsh pressure to Pharaoh's mind and heart, and they will spew out the hatred and malice that is already inside.

As this plays out, Pharaoh becomes increasingly cruel to the Israelites, and God increases the severity of the plagues in order to wield blow after crushing blow to Egypt. After Pharaoh does not bat an eye at Moses' rod becoming a snake, Moses turns the Nile River and all the water in the rivers and streams—and even in jars—to blood. Following Pharaoh's continued refusal, God sends frogs and gnats, to no avail. Then God sends a plague of flies, but keeps them away from His people, the Israelites. No go with Pharaoh. Next, the livestock of the Egyptians are killed. (All livestock in the open fields belonging to the Egyptians die.) Still, Pharaoh refuses. God sends boils to afflict men and animals, and hail to destroy the crops of flax and barley, but still, no release. Then God sends locusts and darkness, but Pharaoh will not budge.

Finally, God sends the plague of death to every firstborn in Egypt. The Israelites have been given specific instructions instituting the first Passover feast, and by obeying God, save every firstborn Hebrew. By marking their doorframes with the blood of the Passover lamb, God identifies them as "His" and death passes by them. This is the event that finally breaks the will of Pharaoh, and he allows the Israelites to leave.

This series of events brings us to an astonishing scene. After consecrating every firstborn to be used for God, including men and animals, the scripture says the Israelites plunder the Egyptians and march out boldly. God is leading them as a pillar of cloud by day, and a pillar of fire by night. Imagine, if you will, 600,000 men, the tally not including women and children, leaving bondage and taking cattle, livestock and the wealth of the Egyptians with them. The total number of people can be estimated between two and three million. What a sight this must have been!

Over the course of days, God leads them precisely where He intends them to go, to the edge of the Red Sea. (Again, this is about two million people, including 600,000 men who are armed for battle.) When Pharaoh realizes he has let the source of all his wealth get away from him, he sends six hundred of his best chariots, along with all the other chariots of Egypt. Pharaoh intends to bring them back into slavery and slaughter a few along the way.

When the Israelites see the chariots bearing down on them, the scripture says they are terrified. In their minds at this very moment, they believe they are dead where they stand; they are caught between the impossible Red Sea and the impossible prospect of fighting the Egyptian army. It would be easy for us to judge the Israelites harshly at this point, but we need to fully understand the scope of the situation. First, in the aftermath of the plagues, there really aren't many chariots left to drive, because many of the horses required to pull them were destroyed. Also, many of the Egyptian soldiers are dead as well, as a result of the plague of the firstborn. The Israelites are now in possession of the

weapons formerly owned by their oppressors, which was received as plunder. There are 600,000 armed Israelite men facing a couple of thousand Egyptian chariots, and the scripture, when referring to original text, says the Israelites were filled with dread and crying in fear.

Fear & Dread

In perspective, we need to understand some things. First, although they possess the weapons, the Israelites haven't had access to them for so many generations that it's a foregone conclusion that they don't know how to use them. They have been *slaves*. No one teaches a slave how to use a weapon. It just isn't done. Second, the Israelites have lived in fear of the Egyptians for good reason. They have been brutally mistreated for so many generations they don't know anything different. Lastly, although they have not seen the power of God working for many years, the God they just experienced through the plagues is a little scary, and completely misunderstood. Of course they're terrified.

Let's also recall that this is an extremely large number of people. Can you imagine a few million people crying out? This is not a quiet whimper. In my estimation, Moses is on the verge of a full-out riot!

Knowing Who's In Charge

Now, Moses makes a statement that is amazing:

> *"Do not be afraid. Stand firm and you will see the deliverance the LORD will bring you today. The Egyptians you see today you will never see again. The LORD will fight for you; you need only to be still." (Exodus 14:13-14)*

This is quite a declaration, friends.

Now, as Moses stretches out his hand, and the Red Sea parts, we are told the Israelites cross over to safety on dry land. Let that settle into your brain. This was not like standing on the edge of the ocean with your feet sinking because it's wet. There was no way to make it across unless it was completely dry. They had carts and buggies with wheels that would've been bogged down, trapping them. Try to imagine what it was like to experience walking this expanse—two or three million with all their belongings—with the view of the walls of sea on either side. God is exerting His power and revealing His providence in a big, big way.

When they are finally across, the pillar of cloud moves across as well, allowing the Egyptian army to pursue them. God makes the wheels of the chariots fall off, then returns the Red Sea to its place, drowning all of them, horses and men alike.

When God said that Pharaoh would pay the price for possessing something that belongs to Him, *this is what He means.* It would do well for us to remember this vision when it looks like everything is against us and there seems to be no way out. Furthermore, this is the type of retribution to Satan that God wants us to envision when we read:

> *"When you were dead in your sins and the uncircumcision of your sinful nature, God made you alive in Christ. He forgave us our sins, having cancelled the written code, with its regulations, that was against us and stood opposed to us; he took it away, nailing it to the cross. And having disarmed the powers and authorities, he made a public spectacle of them, triumphing over them by the cross."*
> (Colossians 2:13-15)

Friends, understand this: we were dead where we stood until Jesus Christ opened the path to salvation and safety, and destroyed sin's hold on us!

Points to Ponder

While it is easy to criticize the Israelite's short memories and their seeming inability to grasp the power and majesty of the God who brought them out of bondage, don't we do the same thing? As a body of believers and as individuals…

- Aren't we equally forgetful?
- Where have you depended on your own limited perception when facing trials?
- When has a personal crisis looked impossible to conquer, or a roadblock looked impassible in the weakness of your vision?
- In which instances specifically have you forgotten to look past your own understanding, and focus on knowing who God is, and the power He possesses?

As we move forward, it will be beneficial to all of us to read and meditate on the words found in Exodus 15:1-18. Here we find Moses singing a song of praise to God. It is the picture of complete gratitude, and the surrender of one's soul to the LORD who saves us from certain destruction.

I will sing to the Lord, for he is highly exalted.
The horse and its rider he has hurled into the sea.
The LORD is my strength and my song; he has become my salvation.
He is my God and I will praise him, my Father's God and I will exalt him.
The LORD is a warrior; the LORD is his name.
Pharaoh's chariots and his army he has hurled into the sea.
The best of Pharaoh's officers are drowned in the Red Sea.
The deep waters have covered them; they sank to the depths like a stone.
Your right hand O LORD was majestic in power.
Your right hand O LORD shattered the enemy.

In the greatness of your majesty you threw down those who oppressed you.
You unleashed your burning anger; it consumed them like stubble.
By the blast of your nostrils the waters piled up.
The surging waters stood firm like a wall; the deep waters congealed in the heart of the sea.
The enemy boasted, "I will pursue, I will overtake them. I will divide the spoils; I will gorge myself on them. I will draw my sword and my hand will destroy them."
But you blew your breath, and the sea covered them.
They sank like lead in the mighty waters.
Who among the gods is like you, O LORD?
Who is like you—majestic in holiness, awesome in glory, working wonders?
You stretched out your right hand and the earth swallowed them.
In your unfailing love you will lead the people you have redeemed.
In your strength you will guide them to your holy dwelling.
The nations will fear and tremble; anguish will grip the people of Philistia.
The chiefs of Edom will be terrified, the leaders of Moab will be filled with trembling, the people of Canaan will melt away;
Terror and dread will fall upon them.
By the power of your arm they will be as still as a stone— until your people pass by.
You will bring them in and plant them on the mountain of your inheritance—
The place O LORD you made for your dwelling,
The sanctuary O LORD your hands have established.
The LORD will reign forever and ever.

Chapter 11

When Faith Is All You Have

Over the years spent sitting at various family tables, and looking back over past experiences and past generations, one thing has become increasingly clear to me. Once you commit to serving Jesus Christ and you walk the walk of faith, there will be times of peace and times of crisis. The peacetime thing is really never questioned. It is meant to be enjoyed, and to a large degree we do. The crisis times, however, are the klutzy stumbles in our otherwise smooth stride, the places where we struggle to find answers in some of life's most excruciating circumstances.

As I have watched my families, both earthly and spiritual, I have observed a few things that have helped me in crisis times of my own, and none more than this one unchanging fact: There comes a moment when you look around and realize faith is all you have. Fortunately this coincides with the exact moment you realize faith is all you need.

What do I mean by this? I mean that in times of devastating loss or in moments of incalculable emotional pain, we realize that God is with us. Abba Father is present not in a sense that the loss or pain is taken away, but that we are not alone and we are loved deeply by The One who never goes away. It's the push that keeps us putting one foot in front of the other, even when things seem hopeless. It's the tiny flicker of flame in our being that assures us that we can face tomorrow, and the next day, and the next. It's the cord that keeps us connected to our Creator, *dropping everything else* and hanging on tightly with both hands.

This deep realization of faith can only come at such times. Certainly we can talk the talk of this faith. But there is no way for us to truly experience such oneness with God until we hit a moment when nothing else can help, which also coincides with the moment of realization that nothing else matters anyway. Certainly one can arrive at a deep faith over time. As a matter of fact, that is the most common way to get there. In hindsight, though, I now completely understand when people warn, "Be careful what you pray for. The path to the answer might not be as easy you think it is."

Like it or not, there is only one express lane to the deepening of one's faith and relationship with God. The kind of faith that moves mountains, I have discovered, is only forged in the fires of profound need, and the only power capable of providing is divine. *Indeed, to experience God in His most memorable work is to see Him come through when the odds are completely against you!*

God's Fast Trackers

The scriptures have many instances in which we can verify this fact. Noah's faith to build the ark, Abraham's faith in the call to sacrifice Isaac, and Moses' faith standing at the edge of the Red Sea are all examples of the type of faith that is forged through the fires of life-threatening need. Looking back at our faith-lineage and those who walked with God before us should truly encourage us as we face our own life-fires.

As we move forward, we can see several notes of importance. Through the power of God, Moses guided the Israelites out of their slavery in Egypt. Through the providence of God, the Israelites crossed the Red Sea to safely escape the Egyptian army

and Pharaoh's wrath. God is accomplishing His purpose for His chosen people, Israel, by leading them to a land He promised their forefathers.

In spite of continual acts of rebellion and unfaithfulness, God still moves forward in His planned purpose for Israel to inhabit a "land flowing with milk and honey." But the Israelite people still cannot fully accept their divine designation, and the blessings, victories and responsibilities that are bound up in that designation. These are shortsighted and fearful people. Because of their disobedience, rebellion and lack of faith, they must wander in the desert forty years, until all those who are unfaithful die, and the next generation replaces them.

During this time, Aaron is gathered to his people and his son replaces him as High Priest. Nearing the end of the forty years, Moses passes his role as leader to Joshua, and then Moses is gathered to his people. God now tells Joshua it is time to take the Israelites into the Promised Land.

The One and Only Hope

As Joshua begins preparations to enter the land God has prepared for Israel, he sends two spies into Jericho to bring back important information that will help them execute God's plan. The spies, though, are found out, but find protection and deliverance at the hand of an unlikely ally. Our story unfolds as the spies enter the city and find their way to the house of Rahab, a prostitute.

> *"By faith the prostitute Rahab, because she welcomed the spies, was not killed with those who were disobedient."*
> *(Hebrews 11:31)*

> *"Then Joshua son of Nun secretly sent two spies from Shittim. "Go, look over the land," he said, "especially Jericho." So they went and entered the house of a prostitute named Rahab and stayed there.*

The king of Jericho was told, "Look! Some of the Israelites have come here tonight to spy out the land." So the king of Jericho sent this message to Rahab: "Bring out the men who came to you and entered your house, because they have come to spy out the whole land."

But the woman had taken the two men and hidden them. She said, "Yes, the men came to me, but I did not know where they had come from. At dusk, when it was time to close the city gate, the men left. I don't know which way they went. Go after them quickly. You may catch up with them." (But she had taken them up to the roof and hidden them under the stalks of flax she had laid out on the roof.) So the men set out in pursuit of the spies on the road that leads to the fords of the Jordan, and as soon as the pursuers had gone out, the gate was shut.

Before the spies lay down for the night, she went up on the roof and said to them, "I know that the LORD has given this land to you and that a great fear of you has fallen on us, so that all who live in this country are melting in fear because of you. We have heard how the LORD dried up the waters of the Red Sea for you when you came out of Egypt, and what you did to Sihon and Og, the two kings of the Amorites east of the Jordan, whom you completely destroyed. When we heard it, our hearts melted and everyone's courage failed because of you, for the LORD your God is God in heaven and on earth below. Now then, please swear to me by the LORD that you will show kindness to my family, because I have shown kindness to you. Give me a sure sign that you will spare the lives of my father and mother, my brothers and sisters, and all who belong to them, and that you will save us from death."

"Our lives for your lives!" the men assured her. "If you don't tell what we are doing, we will treat you kindly and faithfully when the LORD gives us the land."

So she let them down by a rope through the window, for the house she lived in was part of the city wall. Now she had said

to them, "Go to the hills so the pursuers will not find you. Hide yourselves there three days until they return, and then go on your way."

The men said to her, "This oath you made us swear will not be binding on us unless, when we enter the land, you have tied this scarlet cord in the window through which you let us down, and unless you have brought your father and mother, your brothers and all your family into your house. If anyone goes outside your house into the street, his blood will be on his own head; we will not be responsible. As for anyone who is in the house with you, his blood will be on our head if a hand is laid on him. But if you tell what we are doing, we will be released from the oath you made us swear."

"Agreed," she replied. "Let it be as you say." So she sent them away and they departed. And she tied the scarlet cord in the window." (Joshua 2:1-21)

Things are looking bad for the people of Jericho. God has been with the Israelites since they marched out of Egypt forty years before, and their reputation has spread like wildfire. It isn't easy for the complete destruction of the Egyptian army and the loss of property and damage to go unnoticed. In fact, it's impossible because people talk, and folks have definitely told the story about these people and the God they worship.

As the Israelites continue to move towards the land that is promised to them, God provides victory after victory over anyone who opposes His people. Now as they approach Jericho, the spies find themselves in an unnerving situation. Their safety and their fates are in the hands of someone who, according to their standards, is a three-time loser: a woman, a gentile, and a prostitute.

Three Strikes Trust

Try, if you will, to think of how this might be embodied if you were one of the spies. What might someone look like who is your opposite in race, nationality, religion, political affiliation, gender, and lastly… has the worst reputation in town? Then, try to imagine having to trust that person, who according to the evidence is inherently untrustworthy, with the only two things that matter to you: your life and your cause.

What about Rahab? Try to imagine having to choose between the life, people and home you know and the people who have been destroying everyone and everything in their path. These men show up in her place of business, and she is a prostitute so she's used to men in her place of business, but they're not there for a "business transaction." If she reveals them, she's as good as dead; if she is discovered to be hiding them, she's as good as dead. She has to trust people who are her only hope of survival but who also have no reason at all to want to save her. After all, if God were on their side as the evidence has born out, why would they need her at all?

She has to put her trust in those whom she estimates is inherently untrustworthy. Everything is against her, and she has everything to lose.

As we finish the story independently (Joshua 2:15-24, Joshua 6:20-25) and see how both parties keep their word and how Rahab and her whole family are saved, we need to reflect on a few things. First, the scarlet cord is the symbol of a mutually accepted, binding agreement that shows who must be saved from destruction. Had the scarlet cord not been in place, it would have meant her death. That red cord marked who would be saved. Looking back, the blood of the Passover lamb was also a symbol of a mutually accepted, binding agreement. That red blood saved all who were behind the doors where it was marked.

Rahab's decision was far reaching. From examining her story it becomes clear that God honors her faithfulness toward the spies far beyond anything she could have imagined. She could only see the immediate benefit of saving the lives of her family, as noted by the binding oath made with the spies. (Joshua 6:22-25) However, she could not have known that when the laws were given to the people of Israel from God that there were specific mandates

concerning the treatment of foreigners living among His people. In Leviticus 19:33, God states,

> "When an alien lives with you in your land, do not mistreat him. The alien living among you must be treated as one of your native born. Love him as yourself, for you were aliens in Egypt."
> (*Also read Lev 19:16-18; Mark 12:28-31)

When we finally have a complete picture of her life, we see that Rahab is counted among the lineage of Jesus Christ. (Matt. 1:1-17, specifically verse 5) She is also used as a shining example of how faith and works are undeniably linked. (James 2:25-26)

*{*Jesus raises the benchmark concerning LOVE in 1 Cor 13:1-13*}*

One act of faith, marked by a scarlet cord, forever binds Rahab with all those who have walked before us. Together they leave a clearly illuminated path by which we can find the courage and strength to step out in our own declaration of faith, even when everything is against us.

The Tie That Binds

Looking forward to the New Testament accounts of Jesus Christ, we must make a connection.

> "You see at just the right time, while we were still powerless, Christ died for the ungodly. Very rarely will anyone die for a righteous man, though for a good man someone might possibly dare to die. But God demonstrates his own love for us in this: While we were still sinners, Christ dies for us. Since we have been <u>justified by now his blood</u>, how much more shall we be saved from God's wrath through him!" (Romans 5:6-9)

> "Get rid of the old yeast that you may be a new batch without yeast—as you really are. For Christ, our <u>Passover lamb</u> has been sacrificed." (1Corinthians 5:7)

> *"In him we were also chosen, having been predestined according to the plan of him who works out everything in accordance with the purpose of his will…in order that we, who were the first to hope in Christ, might be for the praise of his glory. And you also were included in Christ when you heard the word of truth, the gospel of your salvation. Having believed, you were <u>marked in him with a holy seal</u>, the promised Holy Spirit, who is a deposit guaranteeing our inheritance until the redemption of those who are God's possessions—to the praise of his glory!"*
> *(Ephesians 1:11-14)*

Jesus is the Christ, the Messiah, and the Passover lamb sacrificed for our salvation. His blood by marks the door where inside we will find salvation. His red blood marks those who will be saved. The benefit of choosing Christ is more than far reaching; it is eternal! By his blood, he becomes our brother, and God is our father. Our lineage in the family of God, therefore, is not only linked to Jesus. It is inextricably linked to Rahab as well. Closet skeletons not withstanding, I am proud to be counted among her people.

Points to Ponder

- Where is there "old yeast" in your faith? In other words, what are the influences that prevent you from fully trusting In God, and His power?
- How has your understanding changed concerning the honor and responsibility of carrying God's holy seal, the Holy Spirit, everywhere you go?

Chapter 12

Be Prepared

Have you ever spent a great deal of time in preparation for a special event? I know I have. Every year, I spend several days preparing dishes for Thanksgiving and Christmas. When I was in college, I set time aside to study for tests and exams in order to be adequately prepared. My husband and I spent months preparing for our babies to arrive, and then spent decades preparing them to be ready to leave the nest as independent adults. In preparation for the (ten) moves required by my husband's employment, we nearly perfected the art of purging anything that was old, outgrown or unnecessary for where we would be going, as well as collecting transcripts and records from various schools and doctors to be prepared for any eventuality at our destination. I know many women who literally spent months, even years, preparing for one of the most important days in their lives: their wedding.

The rule of thumb, it seems, is that the more important the event is, the more seriously you focus on preparing for it. There is one person we know, in particular, whose situation required preparation beyond anything I can imagine.

Our family has pseudo-adopted a few treasured people into our fold. One such gentleman is very special to us. He took splendid care of Dad in the last years of his life and also kept a watchful eye on Mom as the Alzheimer's progressed. He was a direct answer to prayer as we tried to prepare for the last-life-stage of the people who had taken care of us before we could care for ourselves. As amazing as his care was, though, that is not the most intriguing thing about him. Our wonderful caregiver is a heart transplant recipient. He has shared his story with me a couple of times, and without revealing his identity, I would like to share it with you.

He had been a caregiver to the elderly parents of some friends of ours, as well as a nanny of sorts to their children. The kids, now older, adore him and still refer to him as their uncle. Several years ago, his health took a turn for the worse, and it was determined that his only hope was a heart transplant. During that time, the family for whom he worked was transferred, and the unanimous decision was that he should stay behind so as to not have to give up his position on the transplant list. Then, to prepare his body to receive what he hoped would come, he went on several drugs and treatments…and waited.

When the call finally came that he would receive a heart, he was relieved and sad all at once, as he completely understood that by receiving his new life, the life of another was lost. More preparations took place—that of the one who would give life, and that of the one who would receive life—so that when the surgery began his new heart could be in his body a rapidly as possible. (Also, imagine the time spent in study by the surgeons preparing them to be able to perform such miraculous healing!) As he tells me often, the rest of his body will give out long before the heart of the eighteen-year-old from whom he was given a new life. He also must be vigilant in the maintenance of his new heart. He takes anti-rejection drugs, and watches for anything that could compromise his health. Something as common as the flu would fight in opposition to his new heart and could kill him. He faces each day with humility and gratitude, and annually takes flowers to the grave of the young man who saved him. As you can see, there was simultaneous preparation of people and

circumstance going on for years before this one, life-changing moment to *receive!*

Preparing God's People for Service to God

As we observed in the previous chapter, God tells Joshua it is time to take the Israelites into the Promised Land. As the God-ordained leader of this people, it is now Joshua who carries the burden of following God's direction and communicating that direction to the people of Israel. God has given very specific instructions concerning how to receive this land, and Joshua must prepare himself and the people to obey fully and completely.

Previously, two spies entered Jericho and were aided by the prostitute, Rahab. She hid the spies from those seeking to intercept them and aided in their escape, ultimately helping them collect all the necessary information that would help the Israelites seize the land. When the spies make their way back to camp, they declare, "The LORD has surely given the whole land into our hands; all the people are melting in fear because of us." (Joshua 2:24)

At this time, Joshua moves the people from Shittim to the edge of the Jordan River. They camp there three days awaiting Joshua's next instructions. They are told, *"Consecrate yourselves, for tomorrow the LORD will do great things among you."* The LORD also tells Joshua that he will begin to exalt him among the people, just as he did for Moses, so they will *know* He is with Joshua just as He was with Moses. The priests are instructed to carry the Ark of the Covenant into the Jordan River. As they do, the waters are cut off, from flood levels to dry land. The people cross over the dry land to the other side, just as they did through the Red Sea, after which a representative from each tribe (12 men) select a stone from the river bed that is then used as a memorial to what God has done for them at the Jordan. There it remains, so that whenever one of their descendants asks about it, the story of God's promise can be told again to each generation. (Joshua 3:1- 4:9)

Now as they await entry to the land, all the men are circumcised, which is the covenant sign of God's promise to this people. This act of obedience must happen before they can proceed into their promised inheritance. It is a non-negotiable regulation of the covenant promise. (Genesis 17:9-14) It is also a requirement for participating in the Passover feast. Four days later they celebrate Passover. The very day after Passover, they eat from the produce of the land that is promised to them. The following day, the manna and quail cease because it is no longer needed.

We now focus on the fall of Jericho. We will examine what it means to follow God's directions, exactly. We will also examine why it is vital that we fully understand what consecration is, and why it holds such importance at this moment.

> *"By faith the walls of Jericho fell, after the people had marched around them seven days."*
> *(Hebrews 11:30)*

> *"Now Jericho was tightly shut up because of the Israelites. No one went out and no one came in.*
> *Then the LORD said to Joshua, 'See, I have delivered Jericho into your hands, along with its kings and its fighting men. March around the city once with all the armed men. Do this for six days. Have seven priests carry trumpets of rams' horns in front of the ark. On the seventh day, march around the city seven times, with the priests blowing the trumpets. When you hear them sound a long blast on the trumpets, have all the people give a loud shout; then the wall of the city will collapse and the people will go up, every man straight in.'*
> *So Joshua son of Nun called the priests and said to them, 'Take up the ark of the covenant of the LORD and have seven priests carry trumpets in front of it.' And he ordered the people, 'Advance! March around the city, with the armed guard going ahead of the ark of the LORD.'*
> *When Joshua had spoken to the people, the seven priests carrying the seven trumpets before the LORD went forward,*

blowing their trumpets, and the ark of the LORD's covenant followed them. The armed guard marched ahead of the priests who blew the trumpets, and the rear guard followed the ark. All this time the trumpets were sounding. But Joshua had commanded the people, 'Do not give a war cry, do not raise your voices, do not say a word until the day I tell you to shout.' So he had the ark of the LORD carried around the city, circling it once. Then the people returned to camp and spent the night there.

Joshua got up early the next morning and the priests took up the ark of the LORD. The seven priests carrying the seven trumpets went forward, marching before the ark of the LORD and blowing the trumpets. The armed men went ahead of them, and the rear guard followed the ark of the LORD, while the trumpets kept sounding. So on the second day they marched around the city once and returned to camp. They did this for six days.

On the seventh day, they got up at daybreak and marched around the city seven times in the same manner, except that on that day they circled the city seven times. The seventh time around, when the priests sounded the trumpet blast, Joshua commanded the people, 'Shout! For the LORD has given you the city! The city and all that is in it are to be devoted to the LORD. Only Rahab the prostitute and all who are with her in her house shall be spared, because she hid the spies we sent. But keep away from the devoted things, so that you will not bring about your own destruction by taking any of them. Otherwise you will make the camp of Israel liable to destruction and bring trouble on it. All the silver and gold and bronze and iron are sacred to the LORD and must go into his treasury.'

When the trumpets sounded, the people shouted, and at the sound of the trumpet, when the people gave a loud shout, the wall collapsed; so every man charged in, and they took the city. They devoted the city to the LORD and destroyed with

the sword everything in it—men and women, young and old, cattle, sheep and donkeys.
Joshua said to the two men who had spied out the land, 'Go into the prostitute's house and bring her out and all who belong to her, in accordance to your oath to her.' So the young men who had done the spying went in and brought out Rahab, her father and mother and brothers and all who belonged to her. They brought her entire family out and put them in a place outside the camp of Israel.
Then they burned the whole city and everything in it, but they put the silver and gold and the articles of bronze and iron into the treasury of the LORD's house. But Joshua spared Rahab the prostitute, with her family and all who belonged to her, because she hid the men Joshua had sent as spies to Jericho—and she lives among them to this day.'
(Joshua 6:1-25)

Be Holy to Receive That Which is Holy

There is so much information within these words, but don't panic or be confused. There is also a common focus in this event, and that is *consecration*. When Joshua tells the people of Israel to consecrate themselves before they begin the move into the Promised Land, he is telling them to *prepare themselves*, to set themselves apart as holy people, in order to *receive* that which was set apart for them by The Most Holy God. In order to receive that which is holy and set apart for them, they must become holy and set themselves apart as a people devoted to God.

In addition, because they have been in the desert forty years, they haven't been abiding by the requirement of the covenant promise: the obedient act of circumcision. Joshua is bringing them full circle, in a sense, reminding them of the holy purpose for which God brought them out of Egypt in the first place: to show all men He is God, the one and only God, who blesses those who follow and obey Him. The physical act of circumcision, which is never outwardly seen, is the mark of identification for God's holy

people. The blessing of receiving the land that was promised to Abraham generations ago is the evidence that can be outwardly seen by all. God brought them out of captivity, when they were unable to escape by any means of their own, and brought them to a place of safety.

On the flipside of this call to be prepared as holy, God commands specific articles to be declared holy and set aside for use by His priests (who are already consecrated to Him, per directions outlined in Exodus 8). Also, everything else is to be destroyed because it is in opposition to Him or was used by those who were disobedient and in opposition to Him. In other words, the people are to remove anything that is in opposition to their designation as God's holy people.

Be Holy, For I am Holy

> *"And a highway will be there; it will be called the Way of Holiness. The unclean will not journey on it; it will be for those who walk in that Way. " (Isaiah 35:8)*

In Joshua 3:5, Joshua declares, *"Consecrate yourselves, for tomorrow the LORD will do amazing things among you."* The word CONSECRATE in Hebrew (*qadas*) literally means holy, sacred. The meaning inferred by consecrate, in reference to man, is that we set ourselves apart in preparation to be devoted to God's holy purpose, that we would function as holy instruments of *Elohim*- His Majesty, Absolute Ruler, Sovereign God. (*Qadas* is a direct derivative of *qodes*, meaning holy or sacred.)

The Israelites have to prepare their hearts, minds and bodies for devotion to God before they can enter into the Promised Land, the land of the covenant promise to Abraham so many generations before. The conditions are made clear, are binding, and are to be fully obeyed in order for the covenant to remain. (Genesis 17) The commands are absolute. They are not to be altered in any way.

The Consecrated, continued...

As we fast-forward into the times of Jesus Christ we find the same meaning within the new and everlasting covenant established through Christ's blood sacrifice. The process by which we prepare our hearts, minds and bodies to receive life in Christ is achieved through repentance, confession, and baptism.

First, *repentance* is the act of leaving our old life behind, just as Abram left his old life behind. It is a turning away from our own way, and a turning towards God's way. After all, how can we receive what God has prepared for us if we are holding onto what we currently have?

Next, *confession* is the act in which we acknowledge we are held captive by sin and are destined to die in that captivity without receiving God's divine intervention: the plan of salvation. This parallels how the Israelites were held captive and could not be set free with out receiving God's intervention.

Finally, through *baptism*, we accept the terms of the covenant established in Christ's death, burial and resurrection. We obey and spiritually legally bind ourselves to this covenant by the physical ceremony of burying our old life in the water, and are resurrected into a new life and family identity where we receive God as our Father, Christ as our brother, and the Holy Spirit as our counselor. *(Rom. 8:29, Eph. 2:14-20, Hebrews 2:11, Col. 2:9-12, Acts 2:36-39)* This parallels how the Israelites faced certain death but passed through the waters of the Red Sea into their new life, leaving their identification as slaves behind and proceeding in their new identity as God's people towards the land promised to them.

Points to Ponder

The circumcision of our hearts is not outwardly seen, but is acknowledged by God as the mark that identifies us as His children. The life we live, as faith becomes manifested within our actions, becomes the outward sign seen by others—the evidence of

our designation as God's holy people—as we wait expectantly for the time when Jesus will come back to take us into our promised land- HEAVEN!

The result should be that we are continually focused on *sanctification*. We should attend vigilantly to the maintenance of our new hearts, making sure that nothing in opposition to God's holy purpose is allowed to compromise our spiritual health. As members of God's household and as bearers of the seal of the Holy Spirit, we must remember that we have been set apart, we have been designated as holy. We have received a divine purpose, which is to actively remain Ambassadors representing the Sovereign Ruler of the land of our citizenship, and to be true representatives of the heavenly territory that is our inheritance.

> *"Therefore, prepare your minds for action; be self controlled; set your hope fully on the grace to be given you when Jesus Christ is revealed. As obedient children, do not conform to the evil desires you had when you lived in ignorance. But just as he who called you is holy, so be holy in all you do; for it is written: 'Be holy, for I am holy.'" (1 Peter 1:13-16)*

- According to the scripture, how do we prepare to receive the grace to be given to us?
- What signs are shown by your actions that you are a member of God's household?
- What are the things in your life right now that could compromise your spiritual health?
- Are there places you've been or things in which you have participated that are inappropriate for someone who bears the seal of the Holy Spirit?
- How might you better represent heaven, the land of your promised inheritance?

Laura Ann Day

Suggested reading:
1 Thessalonians 4:1-12
1 Peter 1:13-23
1 Peter 4:4-12
1 John 1:5-10
1 John 3:1-3
To God Be the Glory!

Chapter 13

The Pictures

Anyone who knows our family knows that we love photography. Walk into any room in our home and you are likely to find photographs of our family. This obsession obviously only goes back a few of generations, as the first photographic pictures weren't made until around 1827, and recreational cameras weren't widely available until around 1900. (Thank you, George Eastman of Eastman-Kodak fame!) The advancement of modern photography, though, has resulted in a multi-generational family clan of photo bugs. Every newborn in our family arrives to dozens of clicking shutters and grows up with the keen understanding that, if asked to smile, it is best to comply. The dereliction of smile duty often results in pictures used for humiliation purposes…*forever*. By the time most have reached their teens, it is completely understood that destroying a photo does no good; somewhere there is a negative, cd or flash drive.

    I have personally accounted for tens of thousands of prints over the years. I can't even fathom how many prints and slides are numbered among the entire lot of us. A point of particular pride is that our granddaughter, Brooklyn, was able to proficiently operate my professional grade digital camera at the age of three. The initial cost of going digital was judged acceptable to my husband only when weighed against the potential savings in film processing. Brooklyn and I are now free to take frame after frame to our hearts' content and can delete anything less than perfect.

Sometimes, though, I just need to hold the pictures in my hands. It would be remiss of me to not carry current photos of our children and grandchildren, and I have been scolded for my failure to produce them in brag sessions. I also carry various sentimental snapshots with me in my Bible, purse, or backpack, depending on where I'm going.

There is good reason for this sappy habit. I want to remember the moment found in the picture. To clarify, it's not just the people in the frame; it's the feelings, experiences and memories—the intangibles within the tangible paper—that are so special to me. The picture is the reminder that it happened. It is the way I keep the people and the moments close to my heart. I carry the pictures because my family really is that important to me. When time, distance or circumstance threatens to cloud my recollection, looking at the pictures always brings me back to the moments we were together.

I enjoy looking at dusty old family albums, squinting to see the faces that left this earth before I met them. The stories that have been passed to me in connection with those pictures are invaluable. They have helped me understand where I came from and strengthened my appreciation for who I am today. My goal is to pass all of them to our children in the hope that they will continue to remember, gaining understanding and appreciation for the past and the present, and then pass them along as well.

The Album of Faith

Remembering has been the whole premise behind this book. By looking though the pictures revealed to us through the stories found in the Bible, we can remember where we came from and appreciate how we got here. We can gain wisdom and

understanding from past events and appreciate the significance of our participation in the present.

By looking back at the beginning of time and the creation of the world, we can appreciate so many different facets of God. The power exuded through His spoken word is awesome and humbling. His ability to design nature with order and the ability to perpetuate itself is astonishing.

Looking back at the beginning of mankind, we can appreciate God's disappointment with disobedience and His heartbreak in separation from us. The pictures we examine through Noah, Abraham and Moses reveal God's love and affection for us even when we lack trust or behave in a manner that does not glorify Him. Thumbing through the images of the Israelites, their desperate captivity, their liberation, their punishment, and finally their inheritance of the Promised Land, we see a God who is faithful to His word, even when we ourselves struggle to be faithful.

In the covenants and promises made by God, we can see Him pointing forward to a time when He would reveal the way for all men to be reconciled to Him. Moving forward and examining the life of Jesus Christ, we see God's shining beacon of hope in a hopeless world!

By connecting the pictures together, we have developed perspective. We see how everything that has happened in the past is related to all the events that followed. We also understand that the time we are in right now is completely connected to all previous times. We see that God has purposefully strung the generations together, like precious pearls along the thread of eternity, each one irreplaceable, and each one lending significant beauty to the whole.

Parting Words

When we sit at God's banquet table and reflect on the family memories of those who walked before us, it truly has been a spiritual feast spread out before us. However, as with every savory meal, there comes a time to conclude.

When we leave our own family gatherings there are many words of encouragement and hugs of thanks generously shared. Those who have plenty always make sure everyone has enough to get them through their journey home. Many times when we were in need, cash was pressed into our hands as we left. We still do the same for our children. The motivation is pure; we want those we care about to have what they need when we aren't physically with them.

We now see that this ritual dates back to the beginning of time. God supplied for the needs of his children when leaving the garden. He supplied what was needed for Noah. He provided amply for Abram and Sarai while they waited for His promise to be fulfilled. He supplied His children, Israel, with manna and quail, even as they were being chastised for their unfaithful attitudes. He has provided food, given protection, and bestows blessings throughout all time.

God's son, Jesus Christ, also addresses the needs of those He is about to leave as we see in the picture of scripture we find in the Gospel of John. His last example, and his last request before accomplishing all he had been sent to do, leaves us memories and experiences for our faith walk, the intangible of the past within the tangible of our present.

The Picture of Humility: The Last Example

First, as he and his disciples prepare to partake in the Passover feast, he rises from the table, ties a towel around his waist, pours water in a basin and proceeds to wash his disciples' feet.

> *"He came to Simon Peter, who said, 'Lord, are you going to wash my feet?'*
> *Jesus replied, 'You do not realize now what I am doing, but later you will understand.'*

> *'No,' said Peter, 'you shall never wash my feet.'*
> *Jesus answered, 'Unless I wash you, you have no part in me.'*
> *'Then Lord,' Simon Peter replied, 'not just my feet but my hands and my head as well!'*
> *Jesus answered, 'A person who has had a bath needs only to wash his feet; his whole body is clean. And you are clean, though not every one of you.' For he knew who was going to betray him, and that was why he said not every one was clean.*
> *When he had finished washing their feet, he put on his clothes and returned to his place. 'Do you understand what I have done for you?' he asked them. 'You call me 'teacher' and 'Lord" and rightly so, for that is what I am. Now that I, your Lord and teacher, have washed your feet, you also should wash one another's feet. I have set you an example that you should do as I have done for you. I tell you the truth, no servant is greater than his master, nor a messenger greater than the one who sent him. Now that you know these things, you will be blessed if you do them.'"*
> (John 13:6-17)

The meaning and application of sanctification is continued here in Jesus' actions. Although Peter objects to having the Lord wash his feet, Jesus is insistent. The meaning of a ceremonial foot washing would be completely understood by these men. They know that the Law of Moses requires the ceremonial washing of the priests' feet and hands before setting about God's business in the temple. The purpose was to set their hands and feet apart for service to God.

Perhaps this is why Peter cries out for his hands and head to be washed as well. Jesus, though, reinforces that they (his disciples) are all already clean; he is showing them that their feet will be taking them places to share the good news of his gospel on God's behalf. Their feet are literally being set apart for God's service. We know they do not fully understand the implications of this action yet but will understand later. He is showing, by personal example, that humility in all things is his way.

The Picture of All-Surpassing Love: The Last Request

Next is Jesus' last request of his Father, as found in the prayer he prays after the Passover feast.

> *"After Jesus said this, he looked toward heaven and prayed: 'Father, the time has come. Glorify your son, that your son may glorify you. For you granted him authority over all people that he might give eternal life to all those you have given to him. Now this is eternal life: that they may know you, the only true God, and Jesus Christ, whom you have sent. I have brought you glory on the earth by completing the work you gave me to do. And now, Father, glorify me in your presence with the glory I had with you before the world began.*
> *I have revealed you to those whom you gave me out of the world. They were yours; you gave them to me and they have obeyed your word. Now they know that everything you have given me comes from you. For I gave them the words you gave me and they accepted them. They knew with certainty that I came from you, and they believed that you sent me. I pray for them. I am not praying for the world, but for those you have given me, for they are yours. All I have is yours, and all you have is mine. And glory has come to me through them. I will remain in the world no longer, but they are still in the world, and I am coming to you. Holy Father, protect them by the power of your name—the name you gave me—so that they may be one as we are one. While I was with them I protected them and kept them safe by the name you gave me. None has been lost, except the one doomed to destruction so that Scripture would be fulfilled.*

I am coming to you now, but I say these things while I am still in the world, so that they may have the full measure of my joy within them. I have given them your word and the world has hated them, for they are not of the world any more than I am of the world. My prayer is not that you take them out of the world but that you protect them from the evil one. They are not of the world, even as I am not of it. Sanctify them by your truth; your word is truth. As you sent me into the world, I have sent them into the world. For them I sanctify myself, that they too may be truly sanctified.

My prayer is not for them alone. I pray for all those who will believe in me through their message, that all of them may be one, Father, just as you are in me and I am in you. May they also be in us so that the world may believe that you have sent me. I have given them the glory that you gave me, that they may be one as we are one: I in them and you in me. May they be brought to complete unity to let the world know you sent me and have loved them even as you have loved me.

Father, I want those you have given me to be with me where I am, and to see my glory, the glory you have given me because you loved me before the creation of the world.

Righteous Father, though the world does not know you, I know you, and they know that you have sent me. I have made you known to them, and they will continue to make you known in order that the love you have for me may be in them and that I myself may be in them.'" (John 17:1-26)

Jesus' prayer is his final time in the throne room with the Father before his betrayal and sacrifice. He is praying for his mission and for the missionaries who will carry his message.

Christ's impassioned requests are both powerful and deeply humbling. He has asked God to guard his followers by putting them *inside his name* at a moment when he is facing the very act that will secure *our place* within his name: death by torturous crucifixion. His time of deep communion with The Father reveals Jesus' desire for his followers to embrace their calling, that of being set apart, as fully and completely as He is about to embrace his own sanctified purpose.

Jesus has shown not only by his entire life-work but especially through the act of washing feet that *complete unity and purpose* may only be found in surrendering to a life of service to The One who holds all power and authority, that is, *Elohim* (God who Reigns), *El'shaddai* (God Almighty), *A'donnai* (Lord and owner of who I am), *Abba* (Holy Father God)! In one resounding crescendo of utter humility and obedience, Jesus forever opens the path for all who follow and obey him to re-establish unity and dependence—the way it was created to be from the beginning of time—and safe haven within the citizenship of heaven. This eternal reward is only accomplished in his death on the cross and triumph over death through his resurrection!

This wonderful, intimate conversation with God reveals how deeply Jesus loves each of us and the urgency he feels to accomplish his mission: Glory to God in a single sacrifice that both justifies and unifies all who choose identification through re-birth in him. As it is written:

> "For no matter how many promises God made, they are 'Yes' in Christ. And so through him the 'AMEN' is spoken by us to the glory of God." (2Cor. 1:20)

In Conclusion

I pray that you will go in peace, and that you will take with you a better grasp on <u>who you are in Christ</u>. I also pray that as a body of believers, we will all find a place of deeper conviction where we joyously accept and embrace the calling for which Jesus prayed so desperately to his Father, *our Father*.

As you take with you the name that is given to you, always remember that your feet carry you as Ambassadors, and Ambassadors are always about the business of The One who sent

them. Praise to God, grace and opportunity to all who follow where His feet will lead.

"How then, can they call on the one they have not believed in?
And how can they believe in the one whom they have not heard?
And how can they hear without someone preaching to them?
And how can they preach unless they are sent?
As it is written,
'How beautiful are the feet of those who bring good news!'"
(Romans 10:14-15)